Black Rodeo in the Texas Gulf Coast Region

Sport, Identity, and Culture

Series Editor: Gerald R. Gems (North Central College)

The *Sport, Identity, and Culture* series addresses the important role sport plays in social, cultural, and political contexts throughout history. While the series is primarily historical in its focus, it welcomes interdisciplinary projects. It is intentionally broad in its conceptualization, as sport—its organization, practice, and meanings—exists both within and beyond the territorial, cultural, social, ethnic, racial, gender, psychological, and chronological borders that construct and define individual and group identity.

Editorial Board
Linda J. Borish, Western Michigan
Susanna Hedenborg, Malmö University
Jorge Iber, Texas Tech University
Malcolm MacLean, University of Gloucestershire
Patricia Anne Vertinsky, University of British Columbia
Gertrud Pfister, University of Copenhagen

Titles in the Series
Asians and Pacific Islanders in American Football: Historical and Contemporary Experiences, by Joel S. Franks
The Miami Times *and the Fight for Equality: Race, Sport, and the Black Press, 1948–1958*, by Yanela G. McLeod
The Early Years of Chicago Soccer, 1887–1939, by Gabe Logan
Transnational Sport in the American West: Oaxaca California Basketball, by Bernardo Ramirez Rios
Sport and the Shaping of Civic Identity in Chicago, by Gerald R. Gems
Black Collegiate Athletes and the Neoliberal State: Dreaming from Bended Knee, by Albert Y. Bimper Jr.
Black Rodeo in the Texas Gulf Coast Region: Charcoal in the Ashes, by Demetrius W. Pearson

Black Rodeo in the Texas Gulf Coast Region

Charcoal in the Ashes

Demetrius W. Pearson

LEXINGTON BOOKS
Lanham • Boulder • New York • London

Chapter 6 reprint: Originally published as "Shadow Riders of the Subterranean Circuit: A Descriptive Account of Black Rodeo in the Texas Gulf Coast Region," by Demetrius W. Pearson, *Journal of American Culture* 27(2) (June 2004): 190–198. Reprinted with permission from John Wiley and Sons. Copyright © 1999–2021 John Wiley & Sons, Inc. All rights reserved.

Chapter 7 reprint: Copyright 2009. From "Black in the Saddle: The Best Bull Rider You Never Saw," by Demetrius W. Pearson, in *Racial Structure & Radical Politics in the African Diaspora, Africana Studies*, Volume 3, pp. 183–196. Reproduced by permission of Taylor and Francis Group, LLC, a division of Informa plc; permission conveyed through Copyright Clearance Center, Inc.

Published by Lexington Books
An imprint of The Rowman & Littlefield Publishing Group, Inc.
4501 Forbes Boulevard, Suite 200, Lanham, Maryland 20706
www.rowman.com

6 Tinworth Street, London SE11 5AL, United Kingdom

Copyright © 2021 The Rowman & Littlefield Publishing Group, Inc.

All rights reserved. No part of this book may be reproduced in any form or by any electronic or mechanical means, including information storage and retrieval systems, without written permission from the publisher, except by a reviewer who may quote passages in a review.

British Library Cataloguing in Publication Information Available

Library of Congress Cataloging-in-Publication Data

Library of Congress Control Number: 2021933835

ISBN: 978-1-4985-7467-9 (cloth : alk. paper)
ISBN: 978-1-4985-7468-6 (electronic)

Contents

List of Illustrations	vii
Preface	ix
Acknowledgments	xv
1 Rodeo Roots and Etiological Aspects	1
2 Land Acquisition in Austin's Colony and Cattle Ranching	11
3 African American Ancestral Involvement and Livestock Management	17
4 The Mythical West: Cowboys, Cattle Drives, and Westward Expansion	23
5 The Emergence of the Black Rodeo Cowboy	33
6 Shadow Riders of the Subterranean Circuit	61
7 Black in the Saddle: The Best Bull Rider You Never Saw	75
8 The New Millennium: Black Rodeo and New Jack Cowboys	91
9 Reliving the Past via Contemporary Trail Riding	105
Epilogue	111
Appendix	113
Index	117
About the Author	125

List of Illustrations

Figure 5.1	Movie Poster, *The Bulldogger*, 1920	34
Figure 5.2	Bill Pickett, 101 Ranch Show	35
Figure 5.3	Jesse Stahl Riding Backward, Pendleton Round-up	36
Figure 5.4	Willie Thomas at Mesquite, TX, '67	42
Figure 5.5	Myrtis Dightman, the Jackie Robinson of Bull Riding with His Statue, Crockett, TX, 2016	48
Figure 6.1	Rodeo Handbill: Trailride and Rodeo	68
Figure 7.1	Willie Thomas on #01 (Beutler Bros.), Tulsa Stampede, 1962	79
Figure 7.2	Bull Rider and Living Legend Willie Thomas, Richmond, TX, 2016	88
Figure 9.1	Prairie View Trailriders Association Logo	107
Figure 9.2	Francies, Dightman, and Cash	108

Preface

This book, in many respects, is the result of my initial visit to a black rodeo as part of some early North American rodeo research conducted at the University of Houston during the 1990s. Prior to this field research, my colleague and I had primarily focused our attention and inquiries on the sociocultural and historical aspects within "mainstream" rodeo, particularly Professional Rodeo Cowboy Association–sanctioned competitions, which received the most print and broadcast media coverage. Unbeknownst to my research colleague and I at the time, I had serendipitously stumbled upon a vibrant, long-standing, circuit of black rodeos and black cowboys who were honing their skills, earning some money, and providing entertainment in one of America's earliest integrated sport forms—rodeo (Rattenbury, 2010). From these early field research visits, which were documented through "research notes," sketches of arenas, 35 mm photographs, videocassette interviews, and memorabilia (e.g., handbills and posters), we found that the remnants and vestiges of previously sanctioned Jim Crow laws and discriminatory treatment had forced black cowboys to create their own rodeos and rodeo organizations. Through the research studies conducted, a detailed circuit of black rodeos scheduled throughout the year that received little to no print or broadcast media coverage was uncovered. They were often staged in small rural environs; the cowboys as well as the vast majority of the spectators were black; and the ancillary aspects or peripheral product(s), in marketing terms, of the rodeo production (i.e., food, music, advertisements, sponsors, etc.) were culturally specific to African Americans.

Over time, I realized there was something very special and unique about what was encountered. It was considerably different from the images and depictions I was most accustomed to growing up conveyed through television, movies, and books. Additionally, it was also somewhat different than mainstream white rodeos that my colleague and I had frequently visited during our previous research studies. To some extent, it appeared that I had traveled back in time and was witnessing a phenomenon akin to the Negro Leagues whereby virtually all individuals associated with the rodeo were African Americans. Wendy Watriss referred to these black rodeos in *Geo* as the "Soul Circuit" (1980, p. 134). I, in turn, viewed them as a "Subterranean Circuit" and dubbed the black cowboys who participated as "Shadow Riders" (Pearson, 2004, p. 102), in a published article for the *Journal of American Culture*, because they basically rode in the shadows of their white rodeo cowboy counterparts, which perceptually rendered them invisible, on a rodeo circuit that appeared to be underground.

Symbolic interactionism served as the conceptual framework and underlying theoretical approach employed to guide the many studies used to write this book and explore the aforementioned phenomenon. Coined by Herbert Blumer in 1937, symbolic interactionism is a sociological concept with a distinctive approach to the study of human group life and human conduct. Originating from the work of George Herbert Mead and other notable contributors, symbolic interactionism attempts to analyze the self-perceptions, meanings, and interpretations of individuals based upon their social interactions. According to Blumer (1969), "the meaning of objects for a person arise fundamentally out of the way they are defined to him by others with whom he interacts" (p. 11). Therefore, people help us define our social world.

This particular theoretical approach was selected because it is emergent, broadly focused, and flexible. Three primary tenets highlight the approach: (1) meanings emerge from social interactions, (2) interpretations of situations emerge from the ways in which people act toward one another with regard to these situations, and (3) the actions of individuals operate in an attempt to define things. In conjunction with the Meadian (Chicago school) tradition of symbolic interactionism, a qualitative research methodology was selected. This research design afforded me the opportunity to immerse myself into the black rodeo milieu without being intrusive, while enabling "key informants" an opportunity to articulate their respective world as they perceived it. The employment of two primary research techniques (i.e., ethnographic and archival), and various data collection strategies, were used to collect information from individuals intimately involved in black rodeos and their respective milieus. This research design helped to accurately recreate, analyze, and discuss the research setting as descriptively as possible.

As noted, this treatise was comprised of ethnographic and archival research. The ethnographic research included individual and group interviews, participant, nonparticipant, and venue site observations; while the archival research component took the form of document and memorabilia examinations obtained from designated libraries, museums, and personal collections. Visits to countless black rodeos, casual conversations with rodeo cowboys and devotees, as well as an extensive literature review over a span of 20 years facilitated the data collection process. Each of these research tools enabled me to collect rich copious amounts of data from sundry sources involved in black rodeo to a point of saturation.

For example, numerous semistructured interviews were conducted with rodeo cowboys/girls, announcers, promoters, stock contractors, judges, bull fighters, concessionaires, and spectators. Their candid statements helped frame the narrative and provided a unique perspective on the inner workings of black rodeo. Access to archived documents and memorabilia housed in various secured locations (e.g., American Cowboy Museum, National Multicultural Western Heritage Museum and Hall of Fame, Black Cowboy Museum, George Ranch Historical Park, etc.) facilitated the research process as both data collection and triangulation sources for cross referencing information found in the field (Pitney & Parker, 2009). The multiple visits to former and contemporary rodeo venues afforded me the opportunity to photograph and/or video record important aspects and nuances within the rodeo production thereby enhancing my ability to recall and recreate salient aspects of the rodeo milieu. This included opening ceremonies and rituals, entry registration procedures, sponsoring entities, concessions, venue physical layouts, and overall rodeo settings. The extensive literature review was instrumental in providing a foundation for this work, as well as a major source for validating information. Lastly, the use of "member checks" whereby designated interviewees were contacted to verify and validate certain information, and secondary sources were invaluable as they enabled me to confirm and disconfirm data obtained in the field. These research procedures helped to enhance the work's reliability and validity. They were critical during the many studies conducted because some of the interviewees were aged with waning memories and the ability to recall specific information was most difficult.

I am truly indebted to, and laud the work of, the many scholars who preceded me in uncovering the true history of the western frontier and the "invisible cowboys," who helped procure and manage a cattle empire in and around the Texas Gulf Coast region that would become second to none. As Jack Weston noted in *The Real American Cowboy* (1985), "By far most early black cowboys came from Texas" (p. 159), which may be referred to as the cradle of black cowboys. These individuals were the ancestors of the rodeo cowboys that I am currently writing about. To date, Texas still has the largest contingent of black rodeo cowboys in the world.

Unfortunately, I will not attempt to name the many scholars whose work provided the impetus, insight, and knowledge for me to undertake this book as I would invariably neglect to list someone who made a significant contribution to this often omitted legacy. Suffice to say, they all contributed immeasurably to the content found in this work. They will not be forgotten.

This book attempts to highlight the etiological aspects and origin of the livestock management industry and the early herders who celebrated their semiannual roundups with fiestas that included *charrería* or what is commonly known as rodeo in Texas. The primary emphasis of the book addresses black rodeo cowboys in the Texas Gulf Coast region from the vantage point of Austin's Colony, also known as the "Old 300" (Roper, Linton, & Hoover, 2019, p. 12), and more specifically the George Plantation/Ranch. This iconic historic site, located in the lush grasslands of Richmond, TX, is still a 23,000-acre working ranch sitting 30 miles southwest of Houston in Fort Bend County. As one of the most profitable settlements within the Old 300, the George Ranch was a Mexican-granted parcel of land that utilized African slave labor to build a cattle ranching empire leading to numerous enterprising spinoff business ventures. It has the distinction of being one of the earliest Anglo settlements in what would become Texas. The George Plantation/Ranch's legacy, in the history of Texas, is undeniable as well as the black cowboys who comprised much of the ranch workforce during its nineteenth-century development.

The history of African Americans in the American West and their cowboy descendants is an enigma in myriad ways. They were a major fixture and stakeholders, who contributed immeasurably to the expansion of the western frontier yet are often marginalized and blatantly omitted from its history in print, film, and artistic renderings. This book addresses some of the many historical oversights and omissions related to nineteenth-century southeast Texas cattle ranching, the long-standing contributions made by black cowboys, and highlights some of the influential individuals who formerly and currently engage in rodeo, as well as its related pastime (i.e., trail riding). A concerted effort has been made to acquaint readers with the role of black cowboys in the cattle industry and livestock management business. Also, their collective voices and experiences have been documented through candid personal interviews and published accounts, as well as their perceived invisibility as ranch hands and rodeo participants in the state most noted for the "cowboy mystique" lore, and bravado.

Within the covers of this book, I contend that the roles and contributions of black cowboys of the nineteenth century, and their twentieth-century rodeo cowboy descendants, have been marginalized, trivialized, and blatantly omitted from the annals of the American West. In essence, they have often been systematically written out of American history and thus relegated to a state of "historical invisibility." Yet, and still, they exist and continue to engage in ranch-related work and play activities through the Soul Circuit/Subterranean Circuit established by them and for them in an ever changing world.

Arriving in the southwestern region of the United States with the Spanish conquistadors in 1528, and having lived in what is known as Texas longer than the Anglo population of the state, African Americans were inextricably instrumental in the development of this vast region despite their invisible status. As enslaved and freed men they intermingled with the Native peoples and Spanish occupiers to create an Afro-Spanish-Indian culture, and where the Spanish went so did blacks. They made up part of the Spanish expeditions throughout Texas, helped build towns, and learned various trades necessary to maintain early frontier settlements in Spanish-Texas. Estevan, the black Moor of Azamor (Morocco) and slave of Captain Andres Dorantes, is noted as being the first black to set foot in present day Texas (Barr, 1996). He was among Pánfilo de Narváez's crew when a storm in the Gulf of Mexico forced the Spanish expedition bound for Florida to seek shelter on an island along the Texas coastline. Adept at learning the languages and signs of the indigenous people, Estevan became a guide more than a slave and traveled throughout Spanish settlements in Mexico and westward into what became Arizona. Other blacks and men of mixed Afro-Spanish-Indian background accompanied Spanish expeditions in East Texas around the late seventeenth century, and often made up part of the garrisons. They would eventually settle in the many Spanish outposts along the Trinity River. San Antonio listed 151 "colored" people among its population around the time the Declaration of Independence was being signed (Barr, 1996). Many of the black people living in Spanish Mexico were born in either Texas or Mexico. Others were escaped slaves who had crossed the Sabine River from Louisiana.

The influx of black Louisiana Creoles in the early nineteenth century contributed to the diverse culture and helped facilitate a burgeoning cattle industry that had developed extensively over the years in an effort to maintain territorial rights and a stable economic commodity. The cattle industry in Texas emerged as the sine qua non economic commodity that shaped the state and created an unmatched ranching culture that spawned a sport form predicated on ranch-related practices.

It is important to note that this work does not attempt to discuss the many black cowgirls that also went up the trail and/or performed over the years in rodeo arenas throughout southeast Texas. Needless to say, they were and are part of the Soul Circuit/Subterranean Circuit living legacy. Nor does it address the infamous black cowboy villains like Dick Glass, Rufus Buck, and Cherokee Bill, who wreaked havoc on the western plains; or the noble peace officers who attempted to bring them to justice like Bass Reeves, Grant Johnson, and Zeke Miller in the historical works of Art Burton in *Black, Red and Deadly: Black and Indian Gunfighters of the Indian Territories, 1870–1907* (1991) and *Black Gun, Silver Star: The Life and Legend of Frontier Marshal Bass Reeves* (2006). However, this book does attempt to fill some of the gaps in our history; uncovers a considerable amount of information on a marginalized group that contributed to the expansion of the American western frontier; and highlights some of the exceptionally talented black rodeo cowboys who, in many respects, were born too early and whose names are rarely found in mainstream rodeo publications, celebratory museums, and halls of fame.

The title of this book, *Black Rodeo in the Texas Gulf Coast Region: Charcoal in the Ashes*, is a sociocultural and historical analysis of enslaved blacks and their descendants who unceremoniously were brought to the Western Hemisphere by the Spaniards (and others) as an unadulterated labor force. Over time they mastered herding and livestock management activities practiced by their captors and indigenous people in Mexican-Texas. Enslaved and freed blacks who were tasked with livestock management duties also engaged in the more festive aspects of the cattle industry. Centuries later they would make an evolutionary transition from mere "boys tending cows" to contemporary rodeo cowboys. Symbolically, "charcoal" represents black cowboys who rodeoed at Soul Circuit/Subterranean Circuit rodeos primarily in southeast Texas before integration, and their engulfment in mainstream rodeos with white cowboys (ashes) since the 1970s. This decade is allegedly when many government-sanctioned discriminatory practices were lifted and Jim Crow laws, which legalized racial segregation mainly in the South, dismantled in many parts of the United States. Thus, America's apartheid form of democracy was called into question by civil rights activists of the prior two decades.

REFERENCES

Barr, A. (1996). *Black Texas: A History of African Americans in Texas, 1528–1995* (2nd ed.). Norman, OK: University of Oklahoma Press.

Blumer, H. (1969). *Symbolic Interactionism: Perspective and Method*. Englewood Cliff, NJ: Prentice-Hall.

Burton, A. (1991). *Black, Red, and Deadly: Black and Indian Gunfighters of the Indian Territory, 1870–1907*. Austin, TX: Eakin.

Burton, A. (2006). *Black Gun, Silver Star*. Lincoln, NE: University of Nebraska Press.

Pitney, W. A. & Parker, J. (2009). *Qualitative Research in Physical Activity and the Health Professions*. Champaign, IL: Human Kinetics.

Rattenbury, R. C. (2010). *Arena Legacy: The Heritage of American Rodeo*. Norman, OK: University of Oklahoma Press.

Roper, C. O., Linton, T., & Hoover, J. A. (2019). *Legacy of the Early Gulf Coast Cowboys*. Houston, TX: Informally Published.

Watriss, W. (1980, December). The soul circuit. *Geo, 2*, 134–150.

Weston, J. (1985). *The Real American Cowboy*. New York, NY: Schocken Books.

Acknowledgments

It was a struggle and pleasure researching and writing this book. The many hours in the field, libraries, museums, and personal collections gave me an unparalleled understanding of rodeo in general and black rodeo in particular. However, nothing was more rewarding than interviewing the many black cowboys over the years and listening to their respective stories and experiences, which have rarely been told and documented. This unique, yet neglected aspect of Western cultural history is vital to our understanding of American society and warrants inclusion. Through my prolonged engagement in the field I vicariously entered the world of the black rodeo cowboy and learned much. From arguably the best and most respected black rodeo cowboy who competed on the Soul Circuit/Subterranean Circuit like the late Willie Thomas, Sr. to the novice competitor at his first rodeo, their stories were compelling and worthy of documenting. I am most appreciative of all the assistance, encouragement, and financial support that enabled this book to be completed. Veteran rodeo cowboys Willie Thomas, Sr., Harold Cash, Cleo Hearn, Freddy "Skeet" Gordon, and Myrtis Dightman, Sr. mentored me throughout the data collection phase by "taking me down the road," opening up their personal collections, and "schooling" me on what used to be. I literally learned from the best. A debt of gratitude goes out to Larry Callies, the owner and curator of The Black Cowboy Museum, for allowing me to examine and scan artifacts from his collection. As a former ranch hand at the George Ranch he was an invaluable resource. Also, a special thanks go out to Dr. Billy Hawkins, at the University of Houston, who encouraged me to undertake this book. Lastly, I would be remiss if I did not thank my family for affording me the requisite time to research and write this book. They were patient and understanding throughout the process.

Chapter 1

Rodeo Roots and Etiological Aspects

North American rodeo has grown exponentially as a contemporary sport form and entertainment option, and for more than a century it has been inextricably tied to the American West. However, prior to rodeo's emergence as the sine qua non form of ranching entertainment during the late nineteenth century, it was already a staple in Mexico due to Spanish conquistadors who brought cattle and horses to the New World in the sixteenth century. The roots of contemporary rodeo or *charrería* can be traced to Mexican bullfighting in the region known as the American Southwest. It is here where the Spanish elite and owners of large haciendas gathered and socialized to watch bullfighting. Rodeo as a cultural athletic pastime increased dramatically among Mexicans when it became open to all social classes (Pearson & Haney, 1999). However, to discuss the genesis of contemporary rodeo a cursory review of the ancient Minoan-Mycenaean civilization may be a viable starting point.

EVOLUTION

Documented as the first European civilization during the Bronze Age (3000–1100 B.C.) on the island of Crete, the Minoan-Mycenaean civilization was known for its taureador sports (Cordes & Ibrahim, 1996; Howell & Howell, 1988; Pointer, 1985). These early sport forms, which consisted of bull vaulting, bull grappling, and various acrobatic bull games, were ritualistic and religious in nature. They were often performed ceremonially during special occasions. The "Taureador Fresco" from the palace at Knossos in Crete, Greece is perceived to be the most dynamic Minoan artifact unearthed to date (Janson, 1995). The fresco appears to depict a young man leaping or vaulting over a charging bull. Although researchers (i.e., ethnoarcheologists,

archeologists, and anthropologists) continue to debate what appears to be depicted in the fresco (Caryl-Sue, 2015), most contend that a leaping maneuver is being performed akin to the modern sport of *Course Landaise* currently practiced in southwestern France and northern Spain.

Upon closer examination of the Taureador Fresco, the trappings of both bullfighting, which includes jumping over charging bulls, and bull grappling, an event similar to modern-day steer wrestling and steer and calf roping are indicative of the ties to North American rodeo. For example, Porter (1985) elaborated on the similarities:

> bulldogging—or steer wrestling as it is now known—possibly predates all of the rodeo contests events. Its roots run to the very dawn of civilization two millennia ago. The bull dancers of Minoan Crete performed a kind of bulldogging, steer wrestling was on the program of the ancient Greek Olympics. (p. 12)

Thus, without question, the Taureador Fresco appears to be the most famous image of bull leaping in antiquity and validates the use of livestock as a quasi-sport pastime.

Bovine-related pastimes albeit much later emerged in northeastern Spain during the thirteenth century in the form of bull running. Originally, it was a practical means for transporting animals from barges or the nearby countryside to the city center. Cattle herders and butchers would clear a narrow strip through town and raced in front of the bulls to guide them to their respective enclosures or bullfighting rings for entertainment and eventual slaughter. The *corrida de toros* or "running of bulls" is most associated with Pamplona, Spain and its San Fermin fiesta (or festival). The roots of this world famous celebratory event dates back to the Middle Ages in the Spanish region of Navarra. Named for the patron saint San Fermin, the herding of bulls to the town pens began well before the festival was conceived. However, the religious facets and the bull runs have merged over time along with the mythical lore surrounding the death of Saint Fermin. The various bull runs, whereby young men seeking to demonstrate their "machismo" and bravado jump into the streets to be chased by herded bulls, have become a cultural tradition prior to major bullfights throughout Spain.

Bullfighting, like bull runs, has also been perceived to be characteristic of masculine Spanish bravado and a cultural staple exported to the many Spanish-occupied territories throughout the Western Hemisphere during the "Age of Exploration." Spanish conquistadores who traveled throughout the New World conquered and colonized numerous lands in Central and South America in such countries known today as Panama, Argentina, Bolivia, Chile, Venezuela, Ecuador, Columbia, and Mexico to name a few. At various times Spain held as many as thirty-five colonies throughout the world.

Where they went so did their culture and cultural pastimes with livestock. The footprint of the Spanish conquistadores on the Southwestern region of what would become the United States of America, and most notably Texas, has had an enduring effect particularly as it relates to livestock management, cattle ranching, and the sport of rodeo. Even though each was practiced in other parts of the country, none would be so inextricably tied to a region. Texas, the once Mexican-occupied territory, eventually became synonymous with livestock management, cattle ranching, rodeo, and cowboys.

MEXICAN ORIGINS

In discussing the cattle industry and livestock management in the Texas Gulf Coast region one would be remiss to overlook the many contributions of Mexican cattle ranching. Brought to the New World as early as the fifteenth century by Christopher Columbus and other Spanish conquistadores, horses, cattle, and mules were among the transported livestock. Cattle would invariably become the sine qua non or lifeblood of the region for centuries to come. Not only was it a major source for beef production; the tallow could be used to make candles, while the hides could be tanned to produce leather products. Thayer Watkins (n.d.) contends that the Franciscans, who were commissioned by the Spanish crown to establish missions to convert the indigenous population to Christianity, introduced cattle ranching and livestock management to the Tejas/Texias community. Because the Franciscans needed an economic base to sustain their community, and encourage settlement to safeguard it from France, they implemented cattle ranching. Mission Indians became the labor force as they were trained in herding tactics predicated on the model of central Mexico (Carlson, 2006). As Jorge Iber pointed out in Paul Carlson's 2006 work, *The Cowboy Way: An Exploration of History and Culture*, the final secularization of missionary facilities after the Mexican Revolution helped provide a surplus of skilled Mexican and American cattle herders for a burgeoning industry.

With an influx of Anglos staking claims in Mexican territories after the 1820s two cattle herding cultures emerged. Surprisingly, many of the new landowners and their cattle herding employees were unfamiliar, forgot, or neglected to acknowledge the skills and techniques initially employed in the industry derived from Mexico. Early Anglo transplants to Spanish Texas owe much to the Mexican herders who taught them the art of herding by horseback. Although they were familiar with cattle raising and herding, it was primarily practiced by foot. Because of the unpredictable nature of nomadic Spanish cattle that roamed the open prairies it was essential to learn the skill of horseback herding. Many cowhands viewed *vaqueros* as the best herders due to their exceptional ability and efficiency in riding, roping, and other essential livestock management skills; particularly those required to handle the cantankerous and often aggressive longhorn cattle during roundups. Anglo ranching by horseback was a gradual process and their reluctance facilitated the employment of Mexicans, Native peoples, and black people to capture and tame wayward livestock. On many Texas ranches as much as 50% of the workforce may have been of Spanish descent. As Carlson (2006, p. 22) noted, "many of the tools, techniques, terms, and much of the culture of the cowboy in the United States, Canada, and even Hawaii can be traced directly back to the Spanish." They were the first individuals to introduce cattle, cattle herding, and cattle ranching as a viable industry in the Western Hemisphere. However, as more Anglos acquired land and gravitated toward the cattle industry the tone, tenor, and image changed, as well as certain cultural perceptions. This was due in part to the mythical legend, lore, and fictional accounts of the Anglo cowboy herder propagated by the many dime novels and baseless artistic renderings of the western frontier. Often depicted in Western movies as evil, corrupt bandits are in stark contrast to the created image that underscores the enduring Anglo cowboy of the Old West. In essence, the name and embodiment of the original cattle herder or *vaquero/charro* was "hijacked" and "whitewashed" since the mid-nineteenth century.

RODEO, A WORK-RELATED PASTIME

The sport of rodeo, which evolved from Spanish herding techniques, owes much to its southernmost border inhabitants in Mexico. Their semiannual roundups of nomadic cattle and horses became celebratory, leading to Hispanic fairs and fiestas that included music, fireworks, dancing, gambling, prayers, and *charrería*—Mexican rodeo. These celebratory occasions which morphed into cultural traditions and the charrería, with its ranch-related competitions featuring horsemanship, roping skills, acrobatic stunts, and pageantry became endemic to the region. Eventually these prole pastimes were emulated and acculturated by transplanted northern immigrants in the form of rodeo.

The emergence of Wild West shows and rodeos unequivocally evolved from the charrería. In addition to the festive atmosphere, events, and trappings of the charrería, adopted by mid-nineteenth-century Anglo ranchers and livestock owners, certain herding equipment, attire, and terminology became associated with the American West lexicon. For example, slick-fork and "open-tree" saddles, unlike the Eastern saddle used by transplant Texans were not readily suitable for cattle herding; thus, many adopted those used by the indigenous Mexican herders of the region. Their saddles were perceived to be better fitting and more comfortable for both rider and animal. The new Texans eventually bought, traded, or learned to make saddles in the likeness of the Mexican herders. Other examples including *herraderos* (branding), branding books, *lazo* (lasso), and lariats; *chaparreras* (chaps), silver-mounted spade bits and spurs; *rancho* (farm), *vaca* (cow), and *vaquero* (cowboy) became western frontier staples. Unbeknownst to most, the prominent North American cattle herders and originators of its proletarian sport competitions were multiracial independent contractors known as *vaqueros*, who were not bound to a ranching hacienda or individual landowner. They were known to be *mestizo*, individuals of Native American and Spanish ancestry, as well as American Indian, African American, mulatto, or *criollo* (Spaniards born in North America). These amalgamated "cowboys" had driven nomadic cattle and wild horses hundreds of years before Texas became the preeminent ranching landscape in North America. Ranching would eventually be the only Spanish institution to survive in Texas and several other western frontier regions.

Although the early settlers to the region learned a considerable amount about the terrain, ranching, farming, and Mexican culture; however, those that came later were not as concerned about the indigenous inhabitants' customs, norms, and mores. As a result, they showed little appreciation and respect. The northern transplants brought their own language, beliefs, and racial biases which considered whites superior to the indigenous people of color. They subsequently ran afoul of Mexican law and opposed the government that ruled the land.

As stated, the semiannual roundup of cattle and wild horses in Mexico, which led to rodeo were part of the inherited cultural traditions and mores of their Spanish ancestors. During the roundups herds were branded, calves earmarked, and bulls castrated. These tasks became celebratory when family members gathered to watch vaqueros engage in these activities which ultimately led to their most revered festive athletic pastime—*charrería*—(or ro-day-o), from the Spanish word *rodear*, meaning to surround or encircle. Thus, the roots of North American rodeo and the national sport of Mexico can be traced to Mexican fiestas in the Southwest.

The Mexican cattle industry with its livestock management tools (e.g., lariats, horned saddles, chaps, etc.) and herding techniques by horseback gave rise to various skill sets employed in competitive ranch-related contests. One such activity that exhibited the trappings of contemporary rodeo was *colear el toro* ("tailing the bull") or the *coleadero*. Similar to steer wrestling, in this contest a skilled horseman chases a bull, grabs its tail, and attempts to flip it to the ground. This extremely dangerous multi-contestant event often injured both man and animal and could last for several hours. Another culturally rooted Mexican charrería event akin to calf roping is the *manganas a caballo*.

Here, a mounted charro lassoes the front legs of a galloping horse to bring it down to the ground in a shoulder roll. This competition, reminiscent of open range capturing of horses for branding, highlights the trick and basic roping skills of the charro. However, the event has recently come under scrutiny by activists claiming "horse tripping" is a form of animal cruelty (Barraclough, 2015). In the same vain is the *piales en lienzo* where the charro attempts to rope the hind legs of a galloping horse. This competition is very much like breakaway roping in mainstream American rodeo, and very much a concern of People for the Ethical Treatment of Animals in various states. Several other ranch-related practices converted into competitive charrería events were the *cala de caballo* (also known as "horse reining") *and jinetas de yeguas*. In the cala de caballo the rider must bring his galloping horse to a stop (preferably a sliding stop), conduct various turns, and back up the animal. These equestrian maneuvers are similar to the cornering of livestock animals and somewhat akin to cutting horse competitions held at contemporary rodeo stock shows. It also demonstrates the charro's ability to handle his animal while the horse shows its expert training. This event may also be likened to the competitive horse competition known as the dressage. The *jinetas de yeguas* was a method used to break wild horses and is essentially bareback bronc riding. Lastly, *jineteos de toros* (bull riding) was also an early charrería event popularized during the early years of the Mexican republic and included in Texas fairs throughout the nineteenth century (Garcia, n.d.). Although not a ranch-related chore it is a fixture in charrería and the signature event in North American rodeos.

Throughout the years there has been an ongoing debate over the origin and use of the term "cowboy." Some contend its roots are in the Spanish lexicon. The Mexican ranch hand, known as a vaquero, is derived from the Spanish word *vaca* meaning cow (Dary, 1989), and is synonymous to the American cowboy. Therefore, a mounted herdsman of cattle was referred to as a vaquero or cowboy in Anglo-American terms. Yet many historians contend the term was coined to denote black slaves, referred to as "boys," who tended to cows on the early farms and ranches. Currently, there does not appear to be a definitive answer regarding the origin of this term, and at certain times during the nineteenth century it was not perceived to be positively regarded. For instance, prior to the mid-1880s cowboy was derogatory slang term meaning drunkard, bum, ruffian, outlaw, and cattle thief. Many did not wish to be called cowboys and preferred to be known as waddys, herders, cowhands, cowpunchers, and wranglers. Those in South Texas preferred to be called vaqueros.

Without question the Mexican vaqueros became an integral purveyor of cattle-related culture in Northern Mexico and "Spanish Texas," through their many contributions to the livestock management industry, yet they along with other marginalized groups were subject to gross discriminatory practices. Even with their advanced cattle herding skills they rarely ascended pass the ranch hand level. Few became foremen or trail bosses.

Vaqueros developed many of the horsemanship, riding, and roping skills associated with rodeo. The most skilled were called charros. These ranch hands were keenly adept at herding and roping, and equipped with various skills that enabled them to entertain at coleaderos and charrearías, specific Mexican rodeos. The charros' use of the lariat to lasso wayward cattle became an invaluable ranching technique that contributed to their exceptional skill set enabling them to entertain audiences with trick roping. Vincente Oropeza, dubbed the fancy roping "Champion of the World" (Rattenbury, 2010, p. 8), is believed to have brought this stylish skill to international prominence when he joined Buffalo Bill's Wild West show in 1894. Oropeza became one of his nation's greatest charros and a pioneer innovator of the Mexican rodeo, as we know it today. The trick roping skill known as *floreo de reata* or making flowers of rope, was originated by charros of old Mexico who were also known for their ostentatious attire when entertaining (Stoeltje, 1989).

Unfortunately, much of the Hispanic rodeo legacy has been marginalized and omitted due to prejudice, according to Mary Lou LeCompte (1985). In *The Hispanic Influence on the History of Rodeo, 1823–1922*, she cites the work of Arnoldo DeLeon, author of *They Called Them Greasers*, who contends that Hispanic fairs and fiestas were not perceived important by Anglo historians even though various sport forms evolved from there. In his words "[They] failed to appreciate their cultural merits and instead identified them with frivolous propensities of Tejanos" (1983, p. 34). Yet, they were much like Anglo fairs and fiestas, and the precursors to American Wild West Shows and rodeos. Allen (1998) may have aptly summed up the plight of Hispanic contributions to North American rodeo in his book *Rodeo Cowboys in the North American Imagination*. He stated:

> Interestingly, and despite his importance in the origins and evolution of the rodeo folk festival, the Mexican American cowboy is the one character who lacks a full-scale artistic treatment in English-language. . . . Racism is certainly a possible factor in the Mexicans' exclusion. . . . (Allen, 1998, p. 177)

Ironically, the Wild West shows of the late nineteenth century were an amalgamation of Western culture in that they were somewhat diverse and inclusive, yet an oxymoron due to their discriminatory aspects. They often included traditional Mexican fiesta pastimes, indigenous Native American pageantry, and various Anglicized rodeo type events including roping, riding, and bronc-busting. "Buffalo Bill" Cody's North Platt, Nebraska, *Old Glory Blow Out* on July 4, 1888, set the stage as other traveling Wild West shows, according to Rattenbury (2010) in *Arena Legacy*, followed shortly thereafter by *Pawnee Bill's Historic Wild West, Colonel Tim McCoy's Real Wild West*, and the *Miller Brothers' 101 Ranch Real Wild West*, to name a few. Bill Pickett, the African American cowboy from Williamson County (Taylor), Texas was a long-time ranch hand on the Miller Brothers' 101 Ranch. The originator of "bulldogging" (steer wrestling), Pickett was a star performer at Wild West shows even though he was often advertised as a Mexican toreador (Pearson, 2009). Ironically, steer wrestling is the only American rodeo event invented by an individual cowboy.

Although there is still debate as to when and where the first rodeo was held, many contend it was at Prescott, Arizona Territory, on July 4, 1888, because of its public advertised admission fee, recorded event winners and times. Subsequently, Prescott rodeo organizers eventually formulated some of the basic rules and attire for competing cowboys. However, the Wild West spectacles staged in the United States and Europe throughout the nineteenth and early twentieth century were the precursor to North American rodeo, which would usurp it as the most widely supported form of Western entertainment toward the end of the nineteenth century.

The North American rodeo, like the Wild West shows that preceded it, attracted a national audience as it toured many northeastern cities subsequently becoming a global export over time. However, much like other sport forms during World War II, rodeo's growth was initially stymied by the mass cancellations of traditionally scheduled competitions and the many rodeo cowboys who enlisted in the armed forces. Baseball was one of the few sport forms mandated by President Roosevelt to continue during the war due to its perceived morale-building effects. Rodeo, as a burgeoning sport form, through its Western-based media outlets (*The Western Horseman* and *Hoofs and Horns*), extolled the virtues of the rodeo cowboy who epitomized bravery, courage, and a no quit persona. Key rodeo officials, like R. J. Hofmann (president of the Rodeo Association of America in 1942) and various military leaders believed the sport could have a "cathartic effect" and engender patriotism through its benevolent acts, civic contributions, and fundraising initiatives. Various patriotic slogans, statements, and depictions of the "soldier-cowboy" image were disseminated nationally and abroad, particularly around military encampments to motivate the troops. Fredriksson (1985) conveyed the prevailing sentiment during the war years:

> During times of stress, there is always a need of some sort of outlet for play and there is a definite need for building up the morale of the people as well as that of the soldiers. Near many cities where rodeos are held are some large cantonments of soldiers, and there is no form of entertainment in the world that pleases soldiers more than rodeo. (p. 70)

It was also implied that cowboys not in the armed services owed it to their rodeo counterparts serving in the military to keep the sport alive in their absence. Civic responsibility was instilled in rodeo cowboys whether they served or not. The deployment of American troops to combat areas throughout the world contributed significantly to the growing appeal and appreciation for rodeo in distant outposts. During World War II rodeos were held in such foreign countries as France, England, Canada, China, Italy, India, and the South Pacific Islands. As a result of its global appeal, image, and war-time contributions, North American rodeo became inextricably linked to patriotism and American values.

REFERENCES

Allen, M. (1998). *Rodeo Cowboys in the North American Imagination*. Reno, NV: University of Nevada Press.

Barraclough, L. (2015, October 22). In defense of Mexican rodeo. *The Los Angeles Times*. Retrieved from http://www.latimes.com/opinion/op-ed/la-oe-1022-barraclough-charro-competition-20151022-story.html

Carlson, P. (2006). *The Cowboy Way: An Exploration of History & Culture*. Lubbock, TX: Texas Tech University Press.

Caryl-Sue, M. (2015, July). Bull leaping. *National Geographic*. Retrieved from https://www.nationalgeographic.org/media/bull-leaping/

Cordes, K. A., & Ibrahim, H. (1996). *Applications in Recreation & Leisure for Today and the Future*. St. Louis, MO: Mosby.

Dary, D. (1989). *Cowboy Culture: A Saga of Five Centuries*. Lawrence, KS: University of Kansas Press.

DeLeon, A. (1983). *They Called Them Greasers*. Austin, TX: University of Texas Press.

Fredriksson, K. (1985). *American Rodeo: From Buffalo Bill to Big Business*. College Station, TX: University Press.

Garcia, M. (n.d.). Charreria. *Handbook of Texas online*. Retrieved from http://www.tshaonline.org/handbook/online/articles/llc04

Howell, M. L., & Howell, R. (1988). Physical activities and sport in early societies. In E. F. Zeigler (Ed.), *History of Physical Education and Sport* (Rev. ed., pp. 1–56). Champaign, IL: Stipes.

Janson, H. W. (1995). *History of Art (Vol. 1)*. New York, NY: Prentice Hall.

LeCompte, M. L. (1985). The Hispanic influence on the history of rodeo, 1983–1922. *Journal of Sport History, 12*(1), 21–38.

Pearson, D. W. (2009). Black in the saddle: The best bull rider you never saw. In J. L. Conyers, Jr. (Ed.), *Racial Structure & Radical Politics in the African Diaspora, Africana Studies* (Vol. 3, pp. 183–196). New Brunswick, NJ: Transaction.

Pearson, D. W., & Haney, C. A. (1999). The rodeo cowboy: Cultural icon, athlete or entrepreneur? *Journal of Sport and Social Issues, 23*(3), 308–327.

Pointer, L. (1985). *Rodeo Champions: Eight Memorable Moments of Riding, Wrestling, and Roping*. Albuquerque, NM: University of New Mexico Press.

Porter, K. W. (1970). *The Negro on the American Frontier*. New York, NY: Arno.

Rattenbury, R. C. (2010). *Arena Legacy: The Heritage of American Rodeo*. Norman, OK: University of Oklahoma Press.

Stoeltje, B. (1989, July). Rodeo from custom to ritual. *Western Folklore,* 48(3), 244–255.

Watkins, T. (n.d.). The origins of the cowboy culture of Western America. *Applet-magic.com*. Retrieved from http://www.sjsu.edu/faculty/watkins/cowboyculture.htm.

Chapter 2

Land Acquisition in Austin's Colony and Cattle Ranching

As previously noted, the threat of French incursion into Spanish colonized territories during the early nineteenth century necessitated the expeditious settlement of American immigrants. Their colony in Matagorda Bay that had been decimated by hostile natives made it imperative for the new republic to welcome nomadic settlers from the east. An enterprising northeasterner named Moses Austin, who was already familiar with Spanish-owned territories in the Midwest during his colonization of lead miners and smelters in Spanish-owned Missouri during the late eighteenth century, took advantage of this opportunity (Moore, 2001). He made a proposal to Spanish officials in 1820 to settle 300 American families in Texas. However, it was initially rebuffed by Governor Antonio Martinez but approved shortly thereafter. Austin's proposed colonization plan eventually fell in the hands of his son Stephen F. Austin due to the elder's death in 1821. Referred to as the "Colonizer" by Tracy and Havelock-Bailie in *The Colonizer* (1941), Austin willingly followed through on his father's enterprise and traveled to San Antonio to gain approval for the proposal. Once affirmed the formation of the colony was announced in newspapers throughout the United States. The initial families who came to Texas as a result of the inducements offered by Stephen F. Austin were mainly from Tennessee, Kentucky, Georgia, Alabama, and Louisiana. Austin's migrant settlers would eventually be known as the "300" or "Old 300" (Roper, Linton, & Hoover, 2019, p. 12). The purchased territory was most expansive. It included the lush prairie lands along the Brazos River in southern Texas, as well as areas near the Gulf Coast (presently Dickinson and League City), and south of Texas City and Moses Lake.

Prospective colonists from various parts of the country sought relocation to Austin's Colony along the lower Brazos and Colorado Rivers. Michael Moore, in Sara Massey's *Black Cowboys of Texas*, noted that this relocation project "... began the first legal settlement of sizeable numbers of Anglo and African families to Mexico-owned Texas" (2000, p. 39). Mexico's National Colonization Law of 1823 enabled settlers to acquire 177 acres for farming and a 4,428 sitio (a "league of land") for raising livestock. The term sitio was used in Spanish Texas to designate parcels of land set aside for specific purposes. Bugbee's comprehensive roster listing of the first families and their respective parcels of land for the General Land Office at Austin was published in the Texas Historical Association Quarterly for October, 1897 (Tracy & Havelock-Bailie, 1941).

Various colonization laws and conditions were mandated by the Mexican government to the prospective settlers. For example: (1) all land had to be improved in two years before a permanent title was issued; (2) land would be tax exempt during the first six years while only half the assessed value of the land would be taxed during the second six-year period; (3) sundry tools and merchandise in the amount of $2,000.00 were deemed duty free at the time the settler took possession of the land; and (4) special consideration was extended to settlers who married Mexican women. Other government restrictions were prescribed by the national decree of August 18, 1824, as well as subsequent provisions passed into law in 1830. Although liberal, to some extent by Mexican government standards, the Austin Colony settlers eventually took issue with the various conditions and mandates imposed. The growing discontentment would ultimately result in the Texas Revolution and the fight for independence.

Stephen F. Austin also had stipulations for those wishing to settle in his colony. He stressed unblemished character, good morals, sobriety, industriousness, and skills sufficient to work a farm. "Frontiersmen" who had no skills other than hunting were strictly forbidden (Moore, 2001). The character of single men was also scrutinized as Austin wanted and actively solicited families, particularly affluent families, who could pay the 12-½ cents per acre land fees. Parcels of land varied based on family size. Therefore, a family with two children could qualify for as much as 1,280 acres at a cost of $160.00. Austin reasoned that this was a bargain compared to the $1.25 fee charged in the United States and would be a means for recouping his family's fortune. Unfortunately, many of the settlers were unable to pay the levied fees. Moreover, as Moore (2001) writes, growing discontentment evolved as affluent settlers as well as family members and friends received more than the standard allotment of land because they could afford to pay their fees in cash. Ironically, land fees were "... payable in cash or Spanish cattle or negro [sic] on receipt of title" (p. 25). Eventually in 1824 the Mexican government instituted a $192 per league fee that annulled the 12-½ cents per acre fee to be paid to Stephen Austin.

Wyly Martin, an early transplant, took full advantage of the league of land offering in present day Brazoria County in 1824. Shortly thereafter he sought additional land for a stock farm in today's Fort Bend County. Henry Jones was another early settler who took advantage of Austin's colonization plan. Neighbors due to the close proximity of their respective plots of land, these two settlers were intimately involved in the employment of African slave labor on their farms and ranches. For example, at times Jones rented slaves from Martin, one of which was Peter who took his master's name and eventually married a slave named Judith owned by Henry Jones. Peter, born in Georgia somewhere between 1800 and 1810, served Wily Martin as a child and accompanied him when he immigrated to Austin's Colony with over 100 head of cattle from Louisiana in 1824 (Moore, 2000).

SLAVE LABOR AND THE MEXICAN GOVERNMENT

During the era of Spanish-governed Mexico, slaves were a precious commodity. Roughly 250,000 African slaves were brought to Mexican territories during colonial times. As William Katz notes in *The Black West* (1996), there were blacks in Texas prior to the arrival of Moses and Stephen Austin. He indicated that a Spanish census from 1792 listed 263 black males and 186 females were among the 1,600 residents of Tejas. Allyn Barr, renown Texas Tech historian and author of *Black Texas: A History of African Americans in Texas, 1528–1995*, elaborated on this point when he stated: "Black people have lived in Texas, though not continuously, for more than four hundred years—longer than in any other section of the United States—considerably longer than the dominant Anglo population of the state" (1996, p. v). He also mentioned that the majority of black people in Spanish Texas were either born in Mexico or Texas.

Thus, the use of African slaves as an indispensable labor force on the plantation–ranches of Martin and Jones proved invaluable, even though the Mexican Congress of 1824 had passed legislation that ended the slave trade. In addition, slavery was illegal in Mexican territories as a result of the Guerrero Decree. Known as Clause 12, it reads as follows: "All inhabitants . . . without distinction of their European, African or Indian origins are citizens . . . with full freedom to pursue their livelihoods according to their merits and virtues" (Vincent, 2001, p. 8). This legislative decree was issued by Vincente Guerrero, former commander in chief of the Mexican army during the latter years of Mexico's war of independence from Spain (1810–1821). His uncanny ability to build coalitions with rival factions helped bring an end to a bitter war. Unbeknownst to many, Guerrero was the second president of Mexico and the first Black Indian president of Mexican territories. He has been regarded by some in Mexican culture as the "greatest man of color" because he championed civil rights (Rivera, 2007, para. 4). In 1829, as head of the "People's Party" in Mexico, Guerrero supported public schools, land reform, and equal rights to all inhabitants. This included disenfranchised African Mexicans and mulattos. Resentment toward his liberal policies by slave traders and illegal slaveholding Texas immigrants, who sought to capitalize on African slave labor, led to Vincente Guerrero's untimely death. As pro-slavery advocates poured into Texas from various parts of the United States, myriad political factions within the Mexican government developed. Eventually reactionaries and conservatives (Bugbee, 1898; Salas, 2018) betrayed Guerrero and overthrew the government within six months of his presidency. During the civil unrest Guerrero was captured and later delivered to Spanish authorities where he was subsequently executed on February 14, 1831. Shortly thereafter slavers initiated a war that would eventually wrestle Texas away from Mexico and permit slavery to continue. This war, known as the Texas Revolution, began in 1835 and culminated in 1836 at the Battle of San Jacinto. The Treaties of Velasco officially gave the Anglos of Texas their independence from Mexico. The General Provisions of the Constitution of the Republic of Texas made slavery legal once again, thereby relegating its African descendent population to Anglo servitude for the next three decades. It also enabled the Anglo-American government to create laws to restrict free black immigration into the republic.

These events boded well for early Austin colonists like Henry Jones, who by 1840 reportedly owned 16 slaves and 800 head of cattle, making him one of the 10 largest stock raisers in the Republic of Texas (Moore, 2000). Although Wily Martin was not as adept at cattle ranching as Jones, their relationship proved to extend much deeper as Martin served as the godfather of Jones's daughter (Polly) in 1826, and shared the cattle herding and stock raising expertise of Martin's slave Peter. It is important to note that Peter Martin was a major contributor to Wylie Martin's ranching success as he managed the plantation and cattle herding businesses.

Thus, the roots of the Texas livestock industry are as diverse as those who herded, branded, and raised the animals. Surprising to many, Louisiana was a major source of the early cattle stock in the Austin Colony. This Spanish-derived breed of cattle roamed and flourished on the prairie land in the southwestern part of the state, as well as southeast Texas. Although the foundation of Western ranching has been hotly debated over the years, scholars tend to agree that the origin appears to reside in Texas. Hispanic ranching culture and customs in *Tejas*, of illegally traded cattle from French settlements like Natchitoches, along with the cultural blending of Anglo-African stock raising techniques created a multicultural industry prior to the Texas Republic. It has been noted that the prairies of southwestern Louisiana played a significant role in the Anglo-Texan ranching industry. Referred to as "originals" by Roper, Linton, and Hoover (2019, p. 12), these individuals had established cattle ranches in South Louisiana well before President Thomas Jefferson made the Louisiana Purchase and Stephen F. Austin arrived in Spanish-held territories with his Old 300 settlers. They were a diverse group of adventurers, migrants fleeing turmoil and war, blacks fleeing slavery, and people seeking a new opportunity. Many of these immigrants became known as "coastal prairie" or "salt grass" cowboys. They contributed to the Texas cattle ranching legacy by capturing and herding feral cattle originally brought to the Southeast region of Texas and Louisiana by Spaniards.

REFERENCES

Barr, A. (1996). *A History of African Americans in Texas, 1528–1995* (2nd ed.). Norman, OK: University of Oklahoma Press.

Bugbee, L. G. (1898). Slavery in early Texas. II. *Political Science Quarterly, 13*(4), 648–668.

Katz, W. L. (1996). *The Black West*. New York, NY: Simon & Schuster.

Moore, M. R. (2000). Peter Martin: A stockraiser of the republic period. In S. R. Massey (Ed.), *Black Cowboys of Texas* (pp. 39–47). College Station, TX: Texas A&M University Press.

Moore, M. R. (2001). *Settlers, Slaves, Sharecroppers and Stockhands: A Texas Plantation-Ranch 1824–1896* (Unpublished master's thesis). University of Houston, Houston, TX.

Rivera, A. (2007, January). Vicente Guerrero (1718–1831). *BlackPast*. Retrieved from http://www.blackpast.org/gah/guerrero-vicente-1783-1831/

Roper, C. O., Linton, T., & Hoover, J. A. (2019). *Legacy of the Early Gulf Coast Cowboys*. Houston, TX: Informally Published.

Salas, M. M. (2018, January 23). Vincente Guerrero—the black president of Mexico. *San Antonio Observer*. Retrieved from http://www.saobserver.com/single-post/2018/01/23/Vincente-Guerrrero-the-Black-President-of-Mexico

Tracy, M. C., & Havelock-Bailie, R. (1941). *The Colonizer: A Saga of Stephen F. Austin*. El Paso, TX: Guynes.

Vincent, T. G. (2001). *The Legacy of Vincente Guerrero, Mexico's First Black Indian President*. Gainesville, FL: University Press of Florida.

Chapter 3

African American Ancestral Involvement and Livestock Management

Historians have long wrestled with the somewhat sketchy details, documentation, and overt omissions in archived sources pertaining to African American involvement in the cattle industry. As historian Deborah M. Liles stated, "[The] use of antebellum black labor is one that is generally overlooked, but it is important when considering the history of black cowboys" (2016, p. 19). The work of John Guice (1977) corroborates this premise as he noted that enslaved African Americans were known for their cattle herding abilities throughout the southern states and Indian Territories. He also mentioned that some early scholars discounted the skills of slaves in the livestock industry, while others acknowledged the significant evidence that confirmed the use of their labor. This has been corroborated through the various letters, journal accounts, and narratives of slaves regarding their bonded servitude. Michael Moore's (2000) research on African American involvement in stockraising during the formative years of Austin's Colony acknowledged the importance of their contributions in elevating this industry to epic proportion. The aforementioned accounts corroborate the work of Texas Tech historian Alwyn Barr, who noted that early Texas cattlemen around the Gulf Coast employed slaves as cowboys to herd cattle, sheep, and hogs. They were also used to break horses. In *Before Emancipation: Black Cowboys and the Livestock Industry* (2016), Deborah Liles stated: "The role of slaves in the livestock industry is vastly underappreciated and rarely acknowledged, as is their participation in the postwar years . . . their place in cowboy history was no less valuable than that of their white counterparts" (p. 27).

It must be clearly stated that cattle herding was not a novel chore for Africans but a mainstay of the subsistence economy in various regions of the African continent well before the colonization of the New World. Cattle herding and dairying were staples in the sub-Saharan areas of Africa albeit done on foot. In the semiarid parts of the region herding was the primary food source because the land was unsuitable for agriculture. Cattle herding in Northern Africa is said to have begun as early as circa 9000 BP (Ryan, Fitts, Muia, Johnson, & Lau, 2009). In eastern Africa cattle herding occurred between 4,000 and 5,000 years ago (M'Mbogori, 2017). Cattle were a precious commodity and far more expensive than sheep, goats, and donkeys because of their multiple uses.

A cow was equivalent to ten goats in value and perceived to be a sign of wealth (Kariuki, 2018). It was also a possession worthy of protecting at all times. Traditionally cattle were used as a bride price in marital negotiations and an ultimate status symbol. As a matter of fact, a special six-foot long stick akin to a contemporary cattle prod was employed so as not to injure the animal. The use of any other stick on cattle was prohibited. Also, specially made cowbells were designed by blacksmiths to keep track of wayward cows and bulls. Cattle were rarely butchered to supply meat. Sheep and goats served as the primary sources of meat. On the other hand, blood, milk, urine, and dung were extracted from live cattle for daily use. When cattle were slaughtered nothing went to waste. Africans found a use for all parts of the animal.

Historically, several of the more notable indigenous cattle herding tribes of Africa include the seminomadic Maasai of southern Kenya and northern Tanzania, the Mudari of the south Sudan, the Tukana of northwest Kenya, the Samburu, and the Fulani. The latter tribe is currently ". . . known to be the largest pastoral, nomadic herding group in the world making them the single 'biggest cowboy tribe' on earth" (Babatunde, 2016). They can be found in west and central Africa, as well as various parts of the Sudan and Egypt. Approximately 13 million Fulani are still nomadic cowboys, and the name has become synonymous with cattle herding for centuries. However, they not only raise cattle but also goats, sheep, chickens, and guinea fowls. Based on this long-standing history of cattle herding it is understandable as to why African slaves from certain regions were more valuable than others.

Prior to the mass immigration of Americans to Spanish Texas (Mexico) African slaves were used as ranch hands in the Carolinas in the late eighteenth century. Both Weston (1985) and Wood (1974) discussed the unique knowledge and skills possessed by African slaves and stated that many white settlers in the Carolinas requested Africans from the Gambian River area. These bonded livestock managers built small cowpens, herded calves, and guarded the stock as they grazed at night. Cattle owners in the South Carolina low country entrusted African slaves to manage large herds, and at times sold their herds and slaves concurrently. The African slave's familiarity with livestock was also noted by historian John D. W. Guice through Louisiana land grant regulations in the 1770s, which required grantees ". . . to be the possessor of one hundred head of tame cattle, some horses and sheep, and two slaves to look after them" (1977, p. 185).

As previously mentioned, Peter Martin was involved in the cattle industry during the early years of Austin's Colony and was among a small contingent of African Texans who owned cattle herds before the Civil War abolished slavery in the state. He was an invaluable asset to his master and the "Texian" army by hunting game and hauling supplies to the front line during their quest for independence from Mexico. Although his master sought to free him from slavery upon his death, the Constitution of the Republic of Texas did not permit freed African Americans to live permanently in the republic. Therefore, Wyly Martin had to seek special permission from Congress for Peter Martin to reside in Fort Bend County. After various appeals and debates over this legal precedence Martin's petition was eventually approved by Congress in 1839, thereby enabling him to remain in Texas. However, his emancipation was not fully formalized until his master's death in 1842.

He became the first emancipated slave legally permitted to live in the Republic of Texas (Moore, 2000). Even though he was a freedman, and one of the top stock raisers in Fort Bend County with over 200 head of cattle and several horses to herd with, his brand was never recorded in the Fort Bend County brand books. Martin's cattle were counterbranded with Henry Jones's daughter, Polly Ryan. During this time, it was customary for African slaves and freedmen to have a white man serve as their guardian due to their social status and limited civil rights. Unfortunately, in spite of his accumulated wealth and the guardians who held the title to his homestead and property in trust, Martin's property disputes would be an ongoing saga throughout the antebellum and post–Civil War period. Greenbury Logan experienced a similar fate in the late 1830s. As a freedman who owned land and livestock, Logan lost his land rights and basically everything once Texas gained independence and was able to freely discriminate and enslave black people. In order to do anything (i.e., collect a debt, purchase land, etc.) he found that the aid of a white person was necessary. Another livestock owning slave by the name of Jim, who was owned by A. Jackson, is believed to be the first African American to record a brand (1831) in San Felipe (Moore, 2000).

In the discussion of livestock management during the formative years of Texas the wealth and influence of Fort Bend County ranchers cannot be overlooked. As one of the initial 300 land grantees, settlers in Austin's Colony had the largest cattle herds in 1845 (Moore, 2000). This included Peter Martin who owned more cattle than the average white stock raiser of the era. However, it was land barons and stockraisers like Henry Jones and Joseph Kuyendall who set the standard. In 1840 their cattle herds ranked them among the top ten ranchers in the state of Texas. Due to their massive herds, Fort Bend County ranked fifth among Texas counties by mid-century and remained one of the principal stockraising centers in the state throughout the nineteenth century (Moore, 2000).

THE GEORGE RANCH: AUSTIN'S COLONY DURING RECONSTRUCTION

The Jones-Ryon plantation (ranch), named after Henry Jones and his son-in-law William Ryon, was the epicenter of the agricultural and livestock management businesses in Fort Bend and neighboring Brazoria County. The actual headquarters of the "plantation-ranch," located in Richmond, TX (Fort Bend County), is where former slave Peter Martin's wife Judith and the Bob Jones family resided as slaves. Martin's long-time relationship with Henry Jones enabled him to use his prairie lands for cattle grazing because Martin did not own any ranching land. He did, however, own a large cattle herd that he eventually sold to acquire property for his family. The descendants of Peter and Judith Martin lived on Martin's Richmond, TX, estate after a bitter court case over his "trusted" land that was sold for Confederate money during the Civil War. With the financial support of Polly Ryon, the case went all the way up to the Texas Supreme Court in 1873, which upheld Judith Martin's claim to her husband's property. The settlement enabled the trust that been created prior to emancipation to be valid and enforceable once slavery was abolished in Texas. "Emancipation Day," known to African slaves in Texas as "Juneteenth," was most beneficial to Judith Martin who was able to inherit her husband's property, and also witness the emancipation of her children. Although few of the children were living at the conclusion of the court case, the descendants of Peter and Judith Martin continued to work in various capacities on the Jones-Ryon ranch lands. For example, George Martin, Peter's grandson worked as a "stock hand" and accompanied trainloads of cattle to market throughout the late nineteenth century (Moore, 2000).

Steve Nelson (2018) highlighted the impact of the Emancipation Proclamation and manumission of formerly enslaved black cowboys in Fort Bend County in an article entitled "A History of Diversity George Ranch Honors Black Cowboy Legacy at First Annual Rodeo" in the *Fort Bend Focus Magazine*. He stated:

> By 1870, there were 76 cowboys in Fort Bend County and 55% of those were black cowboys (with an average age of 24). In many ways, these black cowboys advanced further and faster from slavery's bonds than any others in the county. (para. 8)

Nelson (2018) also noted that their literacy rate was far greater than their peers—"three times greater" and "their personal property ownership was 17 times that of the overall black population" (para. 8).

Such was the case for the Bob Jones family. A slave of Henry Jones for much of his life, Bob Jones became quite prosperous shortly after the abolition of slavery. According to Michael Moore (2000), within three years of his emancipation Jones had the second largest cattle herd among African Americans in Fort Bend County with forty head of cattle and five horses. He eventually expanded his business holdings into cotton and farming. His son Y. Union Jones, who worked as a cowboy for the Ryon Farm and Pasture Company in the 1880s, joined his father in business to form a partnership called Robert H. Jones and Son. Prosperity continued for the family as the younger Jones rented a large farm from the Ryons and turned it into a successful business. By all accounts, he ". . . became one of Texas' most progressive farmers, ranchers and business men, regardless of race or color" (Moore, 2000, p. 44).

The African Texas slave cowboy was a fixture on the Jones-Ryan (eventually George) Ranch, which was inherited by Mamie George in the early twentieth century. The George Ranch, previously referred to as a plantation-ranch in this work, like other early to mid-nineteenth-century agricultural and livestock parcels of land in Texas was a slave-driven facility prior to the emancipation of its African labor force. Many of the African Texas slave cowboys were born on the Jones-Ryan plantation like Peter Martin and Bob Jones. However, black cowboys were a fixture on many of the southeastern Texas plantation/ranches whether they were born in the region or relocated from other parts of the country with their respective slave masters.

Shortly after the Civil War ranch status would be a more appropriate term once manumission of the African slaves occurred. African American cowboys were an invaluable asset and a major factor in the George Ranch's pre- and post–Civil War success. Under the leadership of Polly Ryon, the ranching operations grew exponentially during the late nineteenth century. The estate, valued at $200,000 at the time of her death in 1896, included over 25,000 acres of land and 8,000 head of cattle. The ranch had also diversified in that it now included the Wheat ranch division of the Ryon Farm and Pasture Company. African American cowboys, now working in myriad positions with diverse financial compensation based on skills and performance dominated the labor force. Although a rarity among early cattle drives, ranching, and livestock management in general, some of the cowboys on the George Ranch emerged to such prominent positions as ranch manager, foreman, and "top hand." Moore's extensive examination of the Ryon Farm and Pasture Company payroll records toward the end of the nineteenth century, documented in his master's thesis, revealed the following: "Virtually all of the cowboys shown in pay records of the mid-1890s were African-Americans" (2001, p. 241). This would change dramatically once Mamie George inherited the ranch headquarters in the early twentieth century. Her employment of European emigrant families from Czechoslovakia, Poland, and Germany, as well as Hispanics from South Texas led to the decline of the African American labor force and subsequent black cowboy legacy at the George Ranch. However, early Texas cattle herding and ranching owe much to African slaves and freedmen who worked the ranch for more than a century to make it one of the most financially successful livestock management enterprises in the state, and arguably the most revered pre-republic generational estate.

REFERENCES

Babatunde, M. (2016, September). Africa's indigenous cowboy tribes. *Face2Face Africa.* Retrieved from https://face2faceafrica.com/article/african-cowboy

Barr, A. (1996). *A History of African Americans in Texas, 1528–1995* (2nd ed.). Norman, OK: University of Oklahoma Press.

Guice, J. D. W. (1977). Cattle raisers of the old Southwest: A reinterpretation. *Western Historical Quarterly, 8*(2), 167–187.

Kariuki, E. (2018, April 9). Traditional uses of cattle in Africa. *Owlcation.* Retrieved from, https:/owlcation.com/agriculture/Traditional-uses-of-a-cow

Liles, D. M. (2016). Before emancipation: Black cowboys and the livestock industry. In B. A. Glasrud & M. N. Searles (Eds.), *The American West: On the Range, On the Stage, Behind the Badge* (pp. 19–30). Norman, OK: University of Oklahoma Press.

M'Mbogori, F. N. (2017). Farming and herding in Eastern Africa: Archaeological and historical perspectives. *Oxford Research Encyclopedia of African History.* USA: Oxford University Press.

Moore, M. R. (2000). Peter Martin: A stockraiser of the republic period. In S. R. Massey (Ed.), *Black Cowboys of* Texas (pp. 39–47). College Station, TX: Texas A&M University Press.

Moore, M. R. (2001). *Settlers, Slaves, Sharecroppers and Stockhands: A Texas Plantation-Ranch 1824–1896* (Unpublished master's thesis). University of Houston, Houston, TX.

Nelson, S. (2018, December). A history of diversity: George ranch honors Black cowboy legacy at first annual rodeo. *Fort Bend Focus Magazine.* Retrieved from http://www.fortbendfocus.com/a-history-of-diversity-george-ranch-honors-black-cowboy-legacy-at-first-annual-rodeo/

Ryan, K., Fitts, W., Muia, M., Johnson, N., & Lau, H. (2009). Tracking East African cattle herders from prehistory to the present. *Expedition: The magazine of the University of Pennsylvania, 51*(3), 27–36. Retrieved from https://www.penn.museum/documents/publications/expedition/PDFs/51-3/ryan.pdf

Weston, J. (1985). *The Real American Cowboy.* New York, NY: Schocken Books.

Wood, P. H. (1974). *Black Majority: Negroes in Colonial South Carolina.* New York, NY: W.W. Norton.

Chapter 4

The Mythical West

Cowboys, Cattle Drives, and Westward Expansion

During the great expansion of the western prairie lands and frontier after the Civil War the iconic image of the American cowboy was born. This pioneering individualist whose bravery and guile through the conquest of native people, unchartered terrain, and untamed livestock on the western prairie gave rise to legend, lore, and fictitious accounts. Athearn in *The Mythic West in the Twentieth-Century America* (1986) maintained that "... a mythology with sartorial trappings sprung up" (p. 249). Bruce Glasrud and Michael Searles, in their award-winning book *Black Cowboys in the American West: On the Range, On the Stage, Behind the Badge* (2016), expound on this creation. They contend that the American cowboy has been one of the most idolized, revered, and emulated iconic figures in American history. This archetypal protagonist has served and epitomized an enduring legendary figure in the American psyche.

Dime store novels, bogus accounts, and inauthentic illustrations in the nineteenth century helped create this mythical figure in the minds of generations throughout history. Weston (1985, p. 135) elaborates on what he refers to as "gross anachronisms and historical improbabilities" designed to increase publication profits not necessarily to show what happened. He blames many of the commercial photographers for the scrapbooks, postcard photoprints, graphoscope, and stereopticon cards that were mass produced that rarely included black cowboys. His indictment also included Frederic Remington, the renowned sketch artist of the West, "who painted and sketched many black cavalry soldiers but no black cowboys" (p. 153). Although the criticism may be justified for some American West artists, who neglected to capture the heterogeneity and diversity of the American cowboy, it is not necessarily the case for Remington. His work titled *The Stampede by Lightning* or *The Stampede* (1908), depicting a black cowboy herding cattle during a heavy downpour and lightning bolt, painted shortly before his death in 1909 debunks the criticism of Weston. Yet it is worth noting, according to Harrison (2016), that those tasked with analyzing the aforementioned oil canvas painting through the years have appeared to neglect the black cowboy attempting to quell the stampeding cattle during the storm. Other acclaimed Western artists, namely Will James and Charles Russell like Remington, limited their many drawings and paintings to the Anglo cowboy who would define the "Euro American West" thereby contributing to the mythical protagonist image disseminated throughout the country and perceived as reality through some of the most popular periodicals of the day: *Saturday Evening Post, Ladies Home Journal, Youth's Companion,* and *Scribner's Magazine.*

"From the outset the emergence of the mythic West was a sure thing" (Athearn, 1986, p. 249). Patton and Schedlock's essay entitled *Let's Go, Let's Show, Let's Rodeo: African Americans and the History of Rodeo* (2011) illustrates the impact of "dime novels" featuring cowboys and Indians and the romanticized American West. Numerous factors (i.e., economic frustrations, dreams, east coast conventionalism, nationalism, autonomy, and adventure) nurtured this embellished account of the western frontier. Interestingly, the vast majority of easterners' perceptions were predicated on basic ignorance. They had a vague and unreal perception of the West. Athearn (1986) stated, that their information level hovered near zero; therefore, it was not difficult for them to accept oral reports, largely imaginary, of a legendary land out there. "No one packaged and sold the myth better than William F. ('Buffalo Bill') Cody" (Athearn, 1986, p. 253). Ironically, Cody's lithograph posters and billboards advertising his Wild West shows often neglected to depict black cowboys. Fishwick (1952), opined that the development of the cowboy mythology could also be attributed to rodeo when he stated it had done more to glorify the American cowboy than any other factor, and had "made more cowboys into passing heroes than any other imaginable public spectacle" (p. 86).

However, some chroniclers of the American West opted not to perpetuate the mythical West trope to appease bored and sedate easterners. One Western writer was quoted as stating, "the True West is not always the most appealing of places and suggested that those in search of myth should try Louis L'Armour or Zane Grey" (Athearn, 1986, p. 253). Thus, throughout the years, depictions of the West have literally been a myopic version of "his-story" from an Anglo perspective. As a result, the involvement of other ethnic groups in the expansion and development of the American West (i.e., Hispanics, Native Tribes, and African Americans) has often been perceived as either insignificant or counterproductive to its growth; thus, unworthy of historical significance and documentation.

In the context of this work, African American cowboys were instrumental in the settlement of the West and certainly the movement of cattle from sundry locations in various regions of Texas. Previously delineated, the term cowboy appears to have multiple origins; however, Robbins and Becher (2016) like Newman (1997) stated that it might have first been used in America to denote a black slave's role in the cattle industry. Similar to Peter Martin, who is alleged to have been the first cowboy in Texas, African American cowboys were early stakeholders in the development of the American West in many different ways. Sadly, their involvement and contributions throughout history have often been, marginalized, neglected, and/or blatantly omitted. "The overt omission and trivialization of the contributions made by people of African descent in the expansion of the western frontier has been pervasive and widespread" (Pearson, 2009, p. 184). Albert Broussard's foreword in *Black Cowboys in the American West* (2016) makes note of the fact that African American cowboys remained largely absent from many recreations of the West via fictitious portrayals and embellished tales, a sentiment echoed by Myeshia Babers in her master's thesis where she states: "Their contributions to the building and expansion of U.S. territory and society rivals notions about Black males as lazy and offers counter narratives and representations of Black males' contributions to U.S. society" (2014, p. 25). Lawrence de Graaf, in Bakken and Farrington's *The American West: Interactions, Intersections, and Injunctions (2001)*, contends that the blindness to the Negro in the West was reinforced by standard texts in other areas" (p. 158). Loren Katz, author of the *Black West* shared a similar perspective pertaining to African Americans in print and film when he stated that they have been unceremoniously left out of the history, lore, and legends of the American West. He further noted:

> No phase of our national heritage has been portrayed—in fiction, textbooks and films—as more typically American than the old West. Yet in the hands of the same media this particular slice of Americana has been portrayed as lily-white. (1996, p. xi)

Weston (1985) has been highly critical of the whitewashing of the American West and omission of black cowboys when he states, "This phenomenon of willful exclusion by which those historical images that don't agree with racial stereotypes are deleted from consciousness of generations of Americans deserves further study" (p. 154).

Much like others who sought a better life, African Americans traversed the country on foot, horseback, covered wagon, steamboat, and railroad seeking the American dream. Their exodus from southern slave states to the western plains and mountainous regions required various skill sets unfamiliar to formerly plantation bound slaves. As a result, they became guides, fur trappers, missionaries, stagecoach drivers, blacksmiths, domestics, cooks, chuck wagon drivers, gunslingers, miners, farmers, lawmen, Buffalo Soldiers, and cowboys. De Graaf (2001) points out that many readers of Western history were rarely exposed to the myriad occupations pursued by African Americans before, during, and after the Civil War because many texts and scholarly monographs on blacks in the West rarely ventured west of the Mississippi. The Emancipation Proclamation and the subsequent manumission of African Americans were the impetus leading to their migration west. As such, researchers and historians like Kenneth Marvin Hamilton (1991) and Alwyn Barr (1996) have documented the many black settlements that developed in both Texas and Oklahoma. African Americans created approximately thirty-nine separate communities in fifteen Texas counties at different times in an effort to determine their own destiny. Census data documented by Quintard Taylor (1998), in his book entitled *In Search of the Racial Frontier: African Americans in the American West 1528–1990*, indicates the number of African Americans in Texas far exceeded any other western state or territory. As a result, Texas had more black cowboys than any other state in the nation.

One of the more salient early communities established by black cowboys who worked both the Chisholm and Goodnight-Loving cattle drives was "The Settlement" (Roper, Linton, & Hoover, 2019). Currently located in Texas City, TX, the roots of The Settlement date back to what was a Clear Creek labor camp in north Galveston County in 1864 (Graham, 2014). Once the Civil War ended the land was parceled out for sale in 1867 to many black cowboys who formerly worked for George Washington Butler. Two founding families (the Britton and Phillips) related by marriage, are said to have shortened the name to "Our Settlement" before it was renamed as "Campbellville" after the founder of its first church in the 1870s. Many of the residents of this small community in the early twentieth century were relatives and descendants of the founding families. Even more interesting, "The Settlement boasted an 88% adult literacy rate, and the majority of its residents were landowners" (Graham, 2014, para. 3). In 2010, the *1867 Settlement Historic District* became a landmark and was added to the National Register of Historic Places. To date, it is the only Reconstruction-era historic district in Galveston County. As such, historic markers have been placed at various sites and a restored dwelling of one of its earliest residents serves as a community museum.

HOME ON THE RANGE: BLACK COWBOYS AND THE WESTERN FRONTIER

Former African male slaves, whom had tended plantation-ranch livestock prior to the Civil War, were sought shortly afterwards to round up the nomadic cattle that roamed the lush western prairie lands. Many who chose this occupation found it to be both arduous and dangerous. They were oftentimes summoned to explore mountainous pathways, rescue wayward cattle at night and during inclement weather, or check the depth of waterway passages prior to herd crossings. "Punching" cattle was a better lifestyle for freedmen because they tended to face less prejudice in a highly mobile work-based environment (Barr, 1996). African American cowboys were afforded a modicum of freedom and autonomy on the open range contrary to their counterparts living in rural or urban milieus. Ironically, according to Katz (1996), the less civilized the territory the less racial barriers tended to exist. Those that worked on the storied cattle drives of the era such as the Chisholm and Goodnight-Loving Trails served in many different capacities: wranglers, drovers, ropers, bronc-busters, mustangers, brand readers, and chuck wagon cooks. The early work of Dunham and Jones (1965, p. 291) indicate that African American cowboys were welcomed as "hands" and "top hands," although very few served as trail boss or foreman. Jim Perry, a cook, rider, and fiddler at the renowned XIT ranch was once quoted as saying, "If it wasn't for my damn old black face I'd have been the boss of one of these divisions long ago" (Weston, 1985, p. 152). A white employee agreed, according to Weston (1985), and commented ". . . no doubt he would have" (p. 152). The legendary Texas cattle drives moved livestock from various southeastern locales to western outposts via Oklahoma, Kansas, New Mexico, Wyoming, and Colorado. These distant railway stations (a.k.a. railheads) transported the herds to major markets north and east. Chicago was the most prominent northern destination shortly after the Civil War when Phillip Danforth Armour opened a meat packing plant known as Armour and Company.

As cattle herding cowboys during the post-bellum years, African Americans helped Texas become synonymous with cattle raising and the most prominent beef producer throughout the nineteenth century. African slaves from certain cattle herding regions in Africa like Gambia were adept at livestock management, albeit by foot, but readily acquired the horsemanship, cutting, and lariat skills of the Mexican vaqueros. They were often eager to work in this specialized industry before and after slavery due to its perceived social significance. Unlike slaves, and freedmen who were bound to the land after the Civil War often as sharecroppers, African American cowboys experienced a bit less discrimination with respect to wages, food, and other amenities privy to their white counterparts on the cattle drives.

Regardless of their social status, by no means was the western frontier an inviting oasis for African Americans. As Katz (1996) writes: "the black person who came west, whether slave, slave runaway, or freedman, found neither social mobility, geographical mobility, social acceptance, nor absence of inhibiting customs and laws" (p. 48). Oftentimes African Americans were forbidden to enter a western territory or state due to state/territorial laws and/ or racist townspeople. Katz referred to this discriminatory practice of social segregation as "western colorphobia" (1996, p. 48). However, the cattle industry did enable African American cowboys' employment opportunities rarely experienced prior to emancipation. As a result, they were more numerous in Texas than any other western state or territory (Searles, 2016). African American stock raisers, herders, and drovers also far exceeded their closest rivals in California and Oklahoma (Taylor, 1998). During the late nineteenth century African American cowboys comprised approximately 20–25 percent of the working cowboys in the cattle industry (Barr, 1996). Weston (1985) states:

> Since there were about twice as many black as Mexican cowboys, we can conclude that, on the average, on all the ranges and trails of the Great Plains, of every one hundred cowboys about seventy were Anglos, twenty blacks, and ten Mexicanos. (p.137)

This equates to roughly 5,000–1,200 black cowboys (Durham & Jones, 1965; Nodjimbadem, 2017). Although historians disagree on the approximate figures, Glasrud and Searles in *Black Cowboys in the American West* (2016) contend that the number may very well be in the 8,000–9,000 range as claimed by Porter (1970) and Weston (1985). These numbers and approximations of black cowboy involvement during the height of the livestock management business in the nineteenth century substantiates their presence contrary to the many bogus accounts and depictions of invisibility. For Anglo land barons involved in livestock management this was a fortuitous situation. Not only were black cowboys a viable source of cheap labor in abundance, but depending upon where they were smuggled from Africa or enslaved on the east coast, many were somewhat familiar with herding and cattle ranching techniques. If not, they were amenable to learning the tasks rather than working in the fields. The perception of freedom during slavery, as well as the actual manumission due to the Emancipation Proclamation, afforded black cowboys a modicum of self-destiny and respect. Unfortunately, societal change was inevitable for working cowboys in the cattle industry.

INVISIBLE COWBOYS IN A FADING INDUSTRY

Due to myriad factors occurring around the end of the nineteenth-century America and the American West were transforming socially, economically, and politically. The Industrial Revolution and Reconstruction eras had brought welcomed changes. Communication through Samuel Morse's telegraph invention and later Alexander Graham Bell's telephone made America appear a bit smaller, sending information across the country faster than ever; the railroad system monopolized Cornelius Vanderbilt that transversed the country greatly enhanced passenger travel and facilitated the expeditious transport of freight, including livestock. However, as the economy became more industrialized, and open grasslands became sparse due to the invention and subsequent installation of barbed-wire fencing, cattle drives became an outmoded practice. This along with a massive tick infestation known as "Texas Fever" or the "Winchester Quarantine," which was a fatal disease-carrying bacteria transmitted by South Texas longhorn cattle causing a 95 percent death rate among herds (Deeringer, 2017), brought about a precipitous decline in the Texas beef industry.

Even though longhorn cattle had become immune to the deadly disease, cattle herds in the Panhandle and Midwestern states died within days of exposure. This led to proposed quarantine ranches, spraying or dipping cattle, and vigilantes with loaded Winchester rifles to restrict drovers from transporting South Texas cattle. A fenced trail route over 20 miles wide from South Texas to railway stations in Kansas was also proposed. These prohibitive measures created major problems for South Texas cattle raisers because in some instances ranches were arbitrarily cut in half and separated from water supplies, leading to major armed conflicts between ranchers and the Panhandle Stock Association. This intrastate conflict over the tick infestation and barbed-wire fencing had a major impact on the Texas cattle industry. Martha Deeringer cited a Bureau of Animal Industry report in 1884 that indicated the conflict "enhanced the prejudice against Texas beef, unsettled the trails and markets, agitated the law-making bodies of the West as well as Congress and reduced the consumption of beef" (2017, p. 29). Needless to say, this devastating outbreak stymied the Texas livestock industry and forced many cowboys, white and black, to abandon the cattle drives for steadier ranch work.

Thus, African American cowboys became a faded memory as the twentieth century unfolded enabling white fiction writers and film producers to omit their very presence in the American West. Unfortunately, among those often-forgotten cowboys were cattle herders and ranchers like John Ware, "80 John" Wallace, Jim Perry, and Peter Staples, to name a few. The legendary cattle herding of ex-slave John Ware, who is best known for being the first person to take cattle to Alberta, Canada, is indicative of the salient but often forgotten contributions of African American cowboys. He is currently recognized as the "father" of the livestock industry of Alberta (Texas Cowboy Hall of Fame, Fort Worth, TX, 2017).

Because African American cowboys' livestock management skills were often highly scrutinized, they had to perform their duties better than the average cowboy to gain recognition from white counterparts and ranch owners. This pressure led many to be the best cowhands on the open range. For example, Bill Pickett, the noted Texas-born rodeo performer and inventor of bulldogging (steer wrestling), has been dubbed by some as the greatest cowhand that ever lived (Katz, 1996). This was partly due to his exceptional roping and riding skills. He and his brothers also established themselves as specialists in catching and taming wild cattle and horses, and were known as the Pickett Brothers Bronco Busters and Rough Riders. Similarly, ex-slave Ike Ward was said to be the best roper on the Charles Ward ranch near Goliad, TX (Barr, 1996). As the legendary cattle drives came to an end many of these veteran cattle herders became mentors for young inexperienced cowboys learning ranch life. Some of their students were the sons and relatives of the ranch owners (Howell, 2000).

REFERENCES

Athearn, R. G. (1986). *The Mythic West in Twentieth-Century America*. Lawrence, KS: University of Kansas Press.

Babers, M. C. (2014). *Black Cowboys and Black Masculinity: African American Ranchers, Rodeo Cowboys and Trailriders* (Master's thesis, Texas A&M University). Retrieved from https://oaktrust.library.tamu.edu/bitstream/handle/1969.1/154111/BABERS-THESIS-2014.pdf?sequence=1&isAllowed=y

Barr, A. (1996). *A History of African Americans in Texas, 1528–1995* (2nd ed.). Norman, OK: University of Oklahoma Press.

Broussard, A. (2016). Foreword. In B. Glasrud & M. Searles (Eds.), *Black Cowboys in the American West: On the Range, on the Stage, Behind the Badge* (pp. vii–ix). Norman, OK: University of Oklahoma Press.

Deeringer, M. (2017, September). The Winchester quarantine. *Texas Co-op Power*. Retrieved from https://www.texascooppower.com/texas-stories/history/the-winchester-quarantine

de Graaf, L. B. Recognition, racism, and reflections on the writing of Western Black history. In G. M. Bakken & B. Farrington (Eds.), *The American West, Interactions, Intersections, and Injunctions* (pp. 156–185). New York, NY: Garland.

Durham, P. & Jones, E. L. (1965). *The Negro Cowboys*. New York, NY: Dodd Mead.

Fishwick, M. W. (1952). The cowboy: America's contribution to the world's mythology. *Western Folklore, 11*(2), 77–92. doi: 10.2307/1496835

Glasrud, B. A. & Searles, M. N. (Eds.). (2016). *Black Cowboys in the American West: On the Range, on the Stage, Behind the Badge*. Norman, OK: University of Oklahoma Press.

Graham, C. (2014, March 25). *The Settlement (Galveston County, Texas) (1867–1953)*. Retrieved from https://www.blackpast.org/aaw/settlement-galveston-county-texas-1867-1953/

Hamilton, K. M. (1991). *Black Towns and Profit: Promotion and Development in the Trans-Appalachian West 1877–1915*. Urbana, IL: University of Illinois Press.

Harrison, N. K. (2016). *The Works of Will James: His Contributions to the Mythologizing of the American Cowboy* (Master's Thesis), University of Oklahoma. Retrieved from https://hdl.handle.net/11244/47062

Howell, K. W. (2000). George Adams: A cowboy all his life. In S. R. Massey (Ed.), *Black Cowboys of Texas* (pp. 162–171). College Station, TX: Texas A&M University Press.

Katz, W. L. (1996). *The Black West*. New York, NY: Simon & Schuster.

Newman, A. (1997, September 1). Deep in the heart of Brooklyn, cowboys and kosher food. *New York Times*, p. B1.

Nodjimbadem, K. (2017, February). The lesser-known history of African-American cowboys. *Smithsonian .com*. Retrieved from https://www.smithsonianmag.com/history/lesser-known-history-african-american-cowboys-180962144/

Patton, T. O., & Schedlock, S. M. (2011). Let's go, let's show, let's rodeo: African Americans and the history of rodeo. *The Journal of African American History*, 96(4), 503–521.

Pearson, D W. (2009). Black in the saddle: The best bull rider you never saw. In J. L. Conyers, Jr. (Ed.), *Racial Structure & Radical Politics in the African Diaspora, Africana Studies* (Vol. 3, pp. 183–196). New Brunswick, NJ: Transaction.

Porter, K. W. (1970). *The Negro on the American frontier*. New York, NY: Arno.

Robbins, A., & Becher, M. (2016). *Displacements Exhibition at Museo ICO*. Photographic Journal Exhibit. Madrid, Spain: Museum fur Gegenwartskunst Siegen.

Roper, C. O., Linton, T., & Hoover, J. A. (2019). *Legacy of the Early Gulf Coast Cowboys*. Houston, TX: Informally Published.

Searles, M. (2016). In search of the black cowboy. In B. A. Glasrud & M. N. Searles (Eds.), *Black Cowboys in the American West: On the Range, on the Stage, Behind the Badge* (pp. 211–226). Norman, OK: University of Oklahoma Press.

Taylor, Q. (1998). *In Search of the Racial Frontier: African Americans in the American West 1528–1990*. New York, NY: W. W. Norton.

Texas Cowboy Hall of Fame (2017). *John Ware*. Texas Cowboy Hall of Fame. Fort Worth, TX.

Weston, J. (1985). *The Real American Cowboy*. New York, NY: Schocken Books.

Chapter 5

The Emergence of the Black Rodeo Cowboy

The involvement of African Americans in the sport of rodeo can be traced back to the late nineteenth century. An outgrowth of the Wild West shows, rodeo emerged as a separate entertainment entity. Promotional flyers around the turn of the century, although sparingly, advertised Native American, African American, Hispanic, and female rodeo contestants. Unfortunately, the presence of African American rodeo cowboys would wane in succeeding decades much like other sport forms during the turn of the century. Jay Coakley in *Sports in Society: Issues and Controversies* (2009) contends it was due in part to post-Reconstruction Jim Crow laws that forbid racial integration and the institutionalization of rules prohibiting lower-class involvement in various competitive sport forms. Yet, surprisingly, rodeo will be remembered as one of the earliest integrated sport forms in America.

The two African Americans most associated with the early integration of rodeo are Bill Pickett and Jessie Stahl. Pickett, of black and Cherokee Native American descent, was the second of thirteen children born to former slaves Thomas Jefferson Pickett and Mary Gilbert. A longtime rancher, who had a knack for herding cattle and breaking horses, Bill Pickett was a working cowboy in every sense of the word. At an early age he and his four brothers established a horse breaking business in Taylor, TX. They were known as the Pickett Brothers Bronco Busters and Rough Riders Association specializing in catching and taming wild cattle. Pickett was adept at riding and roping due to his herding days that he became a major box office attraction after signing a performance contract with the Miller Brothers' 101 Ranch Wild West Show in 1907. His celebrity status as the "Dusky Demon" eventually enabled him to star in two motion pictures: *"The Bull Dogger"* and *"The Crimson Skull"* (1921), ultimately becoming the first African American cowboy film star.

Early Western film stars Will Rogers and Tom Mix learned under the tutelage of Pickett and at times served as his assistants.

Pickett's introduction of bulldogging (a.k.a. steer wrestling) to the sport, immortalized in *The Bulldogger*, poster (Figure 5.1), was his signature technique and rodeo-related claim to fame. It is currently the only rodeo event invented by an individual. His rodeo involvement and exhibitions with the Miller Brothers' 101 Ranch Real Wild West Show, which toured many parts of the world around the turn of the century, lasted over 25 years and helped promote his unorthodox method of subduing steer culminated by the cowboy sinking his teeth into the animal's upper lip and raising his hands to show the only grip was with his teeth. This noteworthy accomplishment alone was worthy of his induction into the National Cowboy & Western Heritage Museum (Oklahoma City, OK) in 1971 and the ProRodeo Hall of Fame—Museum of the American Cowboy (Colorado

Figure 5.1 Movie Poster, *The Bulldogger,* **1920.** Ritchey Lithograph Corp, publisher. *Source:* Gift of Jerry L. Murphey, National Cowboy & Western Heritage Museum. 1983.23.

Figure 5.2 **Bill Pickett, 101 Ranch Show.** Unknown, ca. 1925, safety film negative. *Source:* Tad S. Mizwa Collection, Dickinson Research Center, National Cowboy & Western Heritage Museum. 2001.036.024

Springs, CO) in 1989. Pickett, pictured astride his favorite horse Spradley (Figure 5.2), became the first African American rodeo cowboy so honored. The historical marker bearing his name and accomplishments in Taylor, TX, as well as the statue depicting Pickett's bulldogging technique in front of the Cowtown Coliseum in Fort. Worth, TX, are lasting tributes to the legendary cowboy, along with the U.S. Postal Service stamp of Pickett released in 1994 and the California-based invitational rodeo that bears his name.

The plaudits and accolades he received as a working cowboy upon his death in 1932 were equal to his success and fame as a rodeo performer. Zack Miller, owner of the 101 Ranch, referred to Pickett as "the greatest sweat and dirt cowhand that ever lived—bar none" (Katz, 1996, p. 160).

Jesse Stahl, whose place of birth is unknown, was born in 1884. Stahl was an African American ranch hand during the later years of the cattle drives. His uncanny ability to tame and ride "outlaw" horses enabled him to apply his skills to the newly established "sport of the West"—rodeo. Stahl

Figure 5.3 Jesse Stahl Riding Backward, Pendleton Round-up. Ralph R. Doubleday, ca. 1922, photographic postcard. *Source:* Photographic Study Collection, Dickinson Research Center, National Cowboy & Western Heritage Museum. RC2006.116.

would eventually be known as one of the best bronc riders of his time. His legendary ride of "Glass Eye," which had never been ridden in Salinas, CA, in 1912, made him an early rodeo celebrity. Although he rarely won the top prize, many contend it was not due to his riding skills but his skin color. For example, his epic ride of Glass Eye was judged to be third place. In an act of defiance at one particular rodeo, where he was awarded second place, Stahl mocked the judges by riding a second bronc facing backward (Figure 5.3). Similarly, on another occasion he rode the notorious "Tar Baby" backward with a suitcase in hand.

Unbeknownst to many, Stahl is also credited with inventing the rodeo technique and event known as "hoolihanding." The event was similar to bulldogging, invented by Bill Pickett, where a rodeo cowboy leaps from his galloping horse onto the back of a full grown bull, grabbing its horns, and riding the animal until it is tethered by its horns. Several differences existed between the two events. In bulldogging the rodeo cowboy leaps from a galloping horse onto an unleashed steer (young bull) instead of a full grown bull. Second, the cowboy twists the neck of the animal until it surrenders and falls flat on its back. Hoolihanding was subsequently outlawed due to the potential harm to animals and an incident at a California rodeo where a bull broke its neck.

Although not as well-known as Pickett, Stahl was an exceptional bareback rider and bulldogger. However, he eventually moved away from competitive rodeo partly due to the unfair judging and discriminatory practices within the sport to perform exhibitions at traveling rodeos throughout the country. As an exhibition rider he was not subjected to the biased judging and prejudicial treatment by competing rodeo cowboys; thereby assuring him of a steady income. In time, he created exhibition routines with longtime rodeo friend Ty Stokes. They were billed as the "Buckaroo Twins." In a noteworthy exhibition routine dubbed "the outlaw automobile" (O'Hara & Service, 2018), one of the cowboys attempted to rope an animal while the other drove the moving vehicle around the arena. Needless to say, some rodeo enthusiasts consider Stahl to be the greatest bronc rider of all-time. He became the second African American inducted into the National Cowboy & Western Heritage Museum in 1979.

BLACK RODEOS IN THE TEXAS GULF COAST: THE EARLY YEARS

As with most all aspects of American life sanctioned segregation and discriminatory practices (i.e., Jim Crow laws) minimized the opportunities for African Americ vans. Therefore the need to develop their own rodeo circuit was quite evident in that mainstream rodeo competitions routinely conformed to societal norms of the times. This was certainly evident in the sport of rodeo where black cowboys as "solo entrepreneurs" (Pearson & Haney, 1999, p. 324) traveled throughout rural environs oftentimes without any guarantees of lodging, food service, participation, or fair judging and compensation for winning. When they were allowed to compete, it was often in exhibitions, slack contests, or after the main rodeo. The Rodeo Cowboys Association (RCA), which was established in 1936, and its current reorganized (1975) namesake the Professional Rodeo Cowboys Association (PRCA), maintain they have never formally discriminated against blacks (Jackson, 2000; Patton & Schedlock, 2011). However, early black rodeo cowboys state otherwise. Many white rodeo cowboys preferred not to compete with blacks because they believed it was below their dignity. And if, by chance, they happened to lose to a black cowboy the embarrassment would be unconscionable. Therefore, oftentimes they were automatically barred from competing. Even when black rodeo cowboys were able to compete, the biased judging usually minimized their opportunities to win the top prize money, or they may not have been able to collect their winnings at the pay window.

Because of the limited competition opportunities and biased judging in mainstream rodeos, African American rodeo cowboys found it necessary to emulate their black baseball counterparts and establish their own rodeo organization(s) and circuit(s). The Southwestern Colored Cowboys Association, established in the 1940s, was the first rodeo association to organize and sponsor black rodeos. Other such organizations established later included the National Cowboys Rodeo Association (NCRA), Southeast National Cowboy Association (SNCA), All-American Rodeo Association, Anahuac Southwestern National Cowboy Association (SWNCA), and Anahuac Saltgrass Cowboy's Association (ASGCA). The latter association, established in the 1960s, was formed for the express purpose of promoting African American rodeos and is the only one presently in existence. Over time these organizations created a calendar of events that listed rodeo competitions (a.k.a. shows) throughout southeast Texas and Oklahoma from March to November. These shows, which were similar to the many Anglo rodeos known as "pun'kin rollers" (Weston, 1985, p. 154), were often held in small rural environs like Bonham and Sandy Point, TX, primarily for local talent from nearby ranches. The vast majority of the black rodeo cowboys competed on a part-time basis, as very few were able to earn a living competing full time.

The calendar of shows would eventually be dubbed the "Soul Circuit" (Watriss, 1980) by devotees or "Subterranean Circuit" (Pearson, 2004). They included notable rodeo competitions at legendary Texas venues: east (e.g., Dickenson, Raywood, Beaumont, and Liberty), north toward Dallas and Fort Worth (e.g., Madisonville, Fairfield, Crockett, and Fair Park), west (e.g., Acres Home, Navasota, Hempstead, and Plum), and south around Houston (e.g., Fresno, Egypt, McBeth, West Columbia, Richmond-Rosenberg, Kendleton, and Simonton). The most revered rodeo arena of the Soul Circuit/Subterranean Circuit was the Diamond L in Houston, TX, partly because it was black owned, and the first rodeo arena primarily frequented by black cowboys to have RCA/PRCA-sanctioned rodeos. Several of the early sites are currently operational albeit in somewhat disrepair. Yet, they still serve as a viable competition arena and testament to the rodeo organizers, cowboys and devotees that made the Soul Circuit/Subterranean Circuit a meaningful experience.

A pioneering figure in the orchestration of early black rodeo and the Soul Circuit was Floyd Frank. A ranch hand on the McFaddin Ranch, where he learned the skills of a cowboy from his father, is alleged to have established the first African American rodeo in the Anahuac, Texas, area during the 1930s (Wallach, 2016). In the documentary *African American Cowboy – The Forgotten Man of the West* (Lioznyansky, 2013), the plight of black cowboys and their quest to access mainstream rodeo is highlighted. It features Frank, the pioneering black rodeo "architect," as well as mid-twentieth-century notable black cowboys like Willie Thomas, Rufus Green, "Bailey Prairie Kid" Hall, and Myrtis Dightman.

In the mid-1950s Frank built the Floyd Frank Rodeo Arena on his 17-acre homestead in Cheek, TX, which hosted rodeos for close to 50 years. Frank, born in July 12, 1918, may have been the oldest rodeo cowboy of color upon his induction into the National Multicultural Western Heritage Museum's Hall of Fame on July 23, 2016. He was known for training horses, and riding bucking bareback horses. However, Frank is most noted as a rodeo promoter and stock contractor by virtue of his stable of rough stock that included horses, bulls, calves, and steers.

THE CULTURAL CONTEXT OF PARALLEL PATHS

Black rodeo and Negro League Baseball shared a variety of similarities throughout their respective histories. The evolution and etiology of these two sport forms were created as a result of discriminatory practices and sanctioned segregation in a quasi-democratic form of government purportedly based on meritocracy and basic human rights. However, as history notes, this was not the case for various American minority groups that were summarily subjugated, marginalized, and relegated to second-class citizenship. This apartheid form of democracy was prevalent in all aspects of society, including sport. Although African Americans were the largest ethnic minority group for much of the twentieth century (Hobbs & Stoops, 2002), they were literally relegated to a state of invisibility due to their limited access to the spoils of American society.

Sport is an occupation and a form of entertainment like thespian activities that can lead to movies, television, and other forms of visual media. Yet, this occupational pathway was deliberately compromised and distorted by the "white-washing" of American sport figures and the western frontier. Although enterprising black rodeo circuits and Negro League Baseball leagues existed during the early twentieth century, very little media attention was directed toward these sport organizations. However, their subjugated disenfranchised status manifested into a shared kinship, whereby parallel paths within these sport forms developed. Effa Manley, the female co-owner of the Newark Eagles and one of the more successful Negro League franchises, proclaimed that Negro League Baseball was much more than a game and/ or entertainment option. She referred to the sport venue as a "social space" and an environment where civic and community needs could be addressed (Manley & Hardwick, 1976, p. xiii). Such was the case for black rodeos, which were often held in small rural environs devoid of the many civic and entertainment options of larger urban communities. To some extent they continue to fulfill such needs in certain communities.

Prior to the Civil Rights Act of 1964 and 1968, which led to the dismantling of discriminatory policies and government-sanctioned segregation, black rodeos like their Negro League counterparts were salient contributors to the black "eco-system" in their respective communities. For example, at times they were a source of entertainment and pride; a vehicle for seasonal employment; a galvanizing entity for political activism; an economic revenue generator for sport entrepreneurs and small business owners; as well as educational forums. The latter of which has been a major component of the contemporary U2 Production's *Cowboys of Color Rodeo* circuit series. Not only does this nationally renowned minority rodeo circuit pride itself on its entertainment value and high-quality rodeo productions, it also serves as a major educational, historical, and sociocultural purveyor of aspects germane to its minority devotees and those unfamiliar with their contributions to the American West.

THE SOUL CIRCUIT LEGACY

Mid-twentieth-century African American cowboys were primarily relegated to the Soul Circuit even though professional sport integration was underway. Stellar black cowboys, who participated in RCA-sanctioned rodeo competitions, regardless of how well they rode, roped, or steer wrestled rarely won or placed in the money. Unfortunately, according to veteran rodeo observers, it was not due to the lack of talent but often biased judging that prohibited their success and world ranking. Although their names are not listed among the top mainstream rodeo cowboys of their day, several black rodeo cowboys carved out an undeniable legacy that has been resurrected and recorded in various archived documents and repositories. The names of pioneering black rodeo cowboys like Willie Thomas, Rufus Green, Sr., Marvel Rogers, Calvin Greely, Jr., and Myrtis Dightman to name a few tend to conjure up and elicit memories of individuals whose athletic skills exceeded the social norms of their sport and society at large. Sport historians and observers often contend black rodeo cowboys, like the many talented Negro League Baseball players, who were denied the opportunity to compete against white athletes were unfortunately born too soon to fully benefit from their athleticism in a true competitive environment.

Willie Thomas, a veteran Soul Circuit rodeo cowboy of the late 1940s, was born on the legendary George Ranch (formerly Austin's Colony and Jones-Ryan Ranch) in Fort Bend County, TX. He was arguably one of the best bull riders of his day according to veteran rodeo cowboys who witnessed his awesome talent. A collection of letters written by former rodeo cowboys, promoters, announcers, and rodeo devotees extolling his bull riding prowess was read to the audience during his induction ceremony at the Texas Rodeo Cowboy Hall of Fame in 2004. He was the only black rodeo cowboy so honored at the induction ceremony and received a standing ovation from the attendees. Some were not only acknowledging his exceptional bull riding but his grit and courage to do what others chose not to, or would not do, during the Jim Crow era. More recently at the 2019 South Central Texas (SC TX) Rodeo Ring of Honor ceremony Willie Thomas was not only noted as a Black rodeo cowboy pioneer but also referred to as a "bull riding guru" due to his ability to read and anticipate a bull's bucking tendencies. Many bull riders in competition with Thomas frequently sought his advice prior to entering the bucking chute for their respective rides.

As an early African American RCA cardholder, who traveled throughout the United States and Canada, Thomas experienced the cruelty of segregation, discrimination, and unfair judging firsthand. He readily admitted that it was biased judging that often inhibited his rodeo success and necessitated an alternative career choice. Throughout his rodeo career Thomas maintained employment with the Texas Department of Highways, which limited the number of rodeos he could enter and the distances he could travel to compete. In a 2007 interview Thomas lamented about the unfair judging and stated that at times he basically had to ride a bull until it stopped bucking in order to get a reasonable score. "I would have to ride 'em till he lay down" (Pearson, 2009, p. 187). Thomas' best rodeoing years were in the early 1960s when he won approximately $25,000. This was a considerable amount of money for a black man rodeoing prior to and during the landmark Civil Rights Act of 1964, which constitutionally ended segregation in public places and outlawed employment discrimination based on race, color, religion, sex, or national origin.

Years later in an interview with Houston Chronicle correspondent Denny Angelle (1989), Thomas indicated that he was invited to compete in the National Finals Rodeo in 1959 but declined the offer to attend. In retrospect, Thomas regretted his decision: "It was probably the biggest mistake I ever made" (Angelle, 1989, p. C2). His decision not to attend was based on the belief that he would not be judged fairly and subsequently waste his entry fee. In light of the many bull riding buckles, saddles, and financial compensation received by Thomas over the years the National Multicultural Western Heritage Museum and Hall of Fame (MWHMHF) inducted Willie Thomas in the class of 2008. In early 2019 Thomas was honored at the George Ranch, an original site of the "Old 300," with a Black Cowboy Legacy Rodeo. It was a fitting honor for the legendary bull rider who grew up and worked on the ranch. The rodeo, the first of its kind in Fort Bend County, also paid tribute to the many black cowboys who worked the ranch for over 100 years. Krystal Willeby, Director of Programs at the George Ranch, was quoted as stating:

Figure 5.4 **Willie Thomas at Mesquite, TX, '67.** *Source:* Courtesy of Berkley Thomas.

At the George Ranch specifically, four generations of black cowboys worked alongside four generations of the George family, leaving behind a rich legacy of black cowboy heritage that is unique to this part of Texas. The rodeo grew out of the desire to celebrate the skills and contributions of these amazing individuals. (Farrell, 2019)

Unfortunately Thomas, pictured bull riding in Figure 5.4, falls into the same category as many legendary Negro League Baseball players previously mentioned who are deserving of entry into the most prestigious halls of fame, within their respective sport, but may never be inducted because their competition statistics (e.g., annual prize money) were rarely entered into mainstream rodeo ranking systems.

Two often neglected, yet exceptional, rodeo cowboys who took to the rode alongside Willie Thomas during the early years of black rodeo were Sherman Richardson and Clarence Gonzalez. Because of their respective versatility both Richardson and Gonzalez competed in multiple rodeo events. However, they were most noted for their bull riding prowess. Richardson won the bull riding competition at New York City's Madison Square Garden in the early1950s and often competed in the Wild Horse Race Championship like his younger brother, Freddie Richardson. A day camp for children to explore and experience African American history and farm/ranch life in Rosenberg,

TX, has been named in his honor. Gonzalez, like Richardson, was an early RCA/PRCA cardholder and among the first black bull riders to compete in the event at Madison Square Garden. He was also a member of the winning Wild Horse Championship team at Madison Square Garden in 1957 and 1958. Each has been lauded by early Soul Circuit/Subterranean Circuit devotees who watched them, as well as the cowboys who competed against them. Most recently the exceptional rodeo career of Clarence Gonzalez has been acknowledged as he will be posthumously inducted into the 2021 National Multicultural Western Heritage Museum and Hall of Fame (NMWHMHF).

Rufus Green, Sr. is another legendary black rodeo cowboy noted for his superb rodeoing skills but rarely mentioned in the pantheon of great calf ropers. Yet, he became so successful at tie down and break-away calf roping in the 1950s that he quit his ranch job to rodeo full time. This was a bold move for the average rodeo cowboy during the mid-twentieth century, and somewhat foolhardy for an African American cowboy. However, Rufus Green, Sr. was really good. Some contend that he had an uncanny ability to communicate with the horses he rode, roped, and trained. He competed in calf roping events throughout the country and was featured in an *Ebony* magazine story while competing at the Drumright (OK) All Black Rodeo in 1957. Rufus Green, Sr. was not only an exceptional calf roper but at times competed in the all-around competition. According to his NMWHMHF biography, highlighted by Omar Carrizales in the *Handbook of Texas Online* (2013) and Monroe W. Lawson in *Calf Roping With Rufus Green: Fact or Fiction* (1983), he was the All-Around Champion at the Frank County Fair (Ottawa, KS) in 1960 and at Manor Downs (Austin, TX) in 1978. These were major accomplishments in that mainstream rodeos, particularly in the south, were still predominantly white and very few blacks were welcomed to compete.

Rufus Green, Sr. is said to have competed in over 2,000 rodeos during his career. He is not only remembered for his rodeo prowess, that includes the many cowboys and cowgirls he mentored, but also the expert horse training provided for various rodeo events (i.e., roping, hazing, bulldogging, barrel racing, etc.) and ranching activities (e.g., cutting cattle). His early rodeo involvement also enabled him to be one of the founding members of the Southwestern RCA, and among the early black cowboys to receive a PRCA card. Lastly, he was the first African American to compete in the calf roping event at the Houston Fat Stock Show (currently Houston Livestock Show and Rodeo) and placed second in the tie-down competition in 1960. As a sign of the times, this occurred before blacks were permitted to sit in the arena and attend shows on a daily basis. Although deceased, the legacy of Rufus Green, Sr. continues through his veteran calf roping nephew who still competes at Soul Circuit/Subterranean Circuit rodeos while maintaining his horse services business.

Marvel Rogers, an Arkansas transplant and ranch hand with the legendary Beutler Stock Contracting and Rodeo Company, was one of the most colorful rodeo cowboys of his day. Although not a home-grown Texas cowboy, he was a mid-twentieth-century black saddle bronc rider who influenced countless Texas rodeo cowboys. Rogers was a stellar all-around cowboy who made an indelible mark and dubious impression on rodeo cowboys and fans alike. His saddle bronc riding prowess was accentuated by his cigar smoking during the rides. Rodgers is remembered in Michael Allen's *Rodeo: Cowboys in North American Imagination* (1998, p. 181), as "the greatest natural-born saddle bronc rider I ever saw." A close friend of Marvel Rogers, Pro Rodeo Hall of Fame inductee Harry Thompkins, believed that he was often unfairly judged at rodeos. Wayne Wooden and Gavin Ehringer in *Rodeo in America* (1996, p. 208) quote Thompkins as stating, "Rogers was the most-robbed cowboy in rodeo," a quote echoed in an interview with his longtime mentee Cleo Hern (personal communication, May 20, 2019). In spite of his limited success in mainstream rodeo competitions, he was a legend and major money winner on the black rodeo circuits in Texas and Oklahoma. Hearn, a protégée of Rogers and an early black calf roper, recalls the "hat rides" which were customary at black rodeos during the days of segregated rodeos. He maintains that hat rides were often instituted primarily to see Rogers ride. Ironically, some were said to payout more than the top prize money at regular rodeos, a statement corroborated by other cowboys of the day.

Like Rogers, and other mid-twentieth-century notable black rodeo cowboys, Calvin Greely, Jr. was a consummate all-around rodeo cowboy who was born a bit too soon. He was an early black PRCA cardholder of the 1950s who was relegated to the pre- and post-rodeo competitions because of his skin color. In spite of this customary discriminatory slight Greely excelled. A Rufus Green, Sr. protégé, Greely competed in rodeo competitions in the United States and Canada winning numerous saddles and belt buckles. He is credited as having won twelve calf roping and steer wrestling championships. Unfortunately, during his rodeo career Greely had to maintain steady employment as a truck driver and rodeo when he could. This fact of life minimized his visibility, PRCA rankings, and career earning potential. However, throughout his rodeo career Greely was an inspiration and mentor to up and coming calf ropers. PRCA World Champion calf ropers Fred Whitfield and Joe Beavers can attest to his mentorship. They both learned from Greely, and Beavers even had roping horses trained by him. Greely has been lauded over the years for his efforts to increase the percentage of African American cowboys in the PRCA. He was a member of numerous rodeo associations and organizations established to increase African American involvement in the sport of rodeo. Calvin Greeley, Jr. was inducted into both the NMWHMHF (2009), as well as the Texas Rodeo Cowboy Hall of Fame (2016).

Arguably one of the least celebrated champion bull riders of the Soul Circuit/Subterranean Circuit during the mid-1950s and 1960s was Clinton Wyche (pronounced "Worth"). He was known to rodeo devotees in and around southeast Texas as one of the most talented bull riders regardless of color. Larry Callies, curator of The Black Cowboy Museum and former rodeo cowboy, stated Wyche could have won the World Bull Riding Championship had he chose to go down the road and rodeo full time. Wyche, a consummate family man, who chose domestic obligations over possible rodeo success, found his niche at rodeo competitions primarily in Texas. He won the first bull riding competition he entered at the T-Diamond Ranch in West Columbia, TX, according to his son, who accepted a plaque and commemorative belt buckle on behalf of his father at the South Central Texas (SC TX) Rodeo Ring of Honor induction ceremony in 2019. Wyche was inducted posthumously for his bull riding talents. His induction ceremony backdrop on the video screen read as follows: "1968 Championship – History In The Making: Black Cowboy Winning A Rodeo Championship In A Predominantly White Rodeo Association" (SC TX, 2019).

Without question the most celebrated black rodeo cowboy of the Soul Circuit/Subterranean Circuit has to be Myrtis Dightman. Although his fame and notoriety have come recently, those that were privy to see him ride know it is a long overdue honor. Referred to as the "Jackie Robinson of Rodeo" by Christian Wallace in a *Texas Monthly* (2018) magazine feature story entitled "The Greatest," Dightman is credited as the first black rodeo cowboy to qualify for the National Finals Rodeo in 1966. The following year he became the number one ranked bull rider in the world and the first African American to hold such an honor. Dightman ended the 1967 season third in the official world standings. His 20-plus years of bull riding actually started late as he did not take up the event until the age of 25. He initially started as a bullfighter (a.k.a. rodeo clown) in rodeos around Houston, TX.

Dightman was arguably the only African American competing full time on the RCA circuit during the 1960s, a time when very few black rodeo cowboys competed in RCA-sanctioned rodeos. As mentioned in various RCA (and PRCA) documents, there was never any definitive position that mandated the exclusion of African Americans from their rodeos; however, there never appeared to be a warm and open welcome extended to black rodeo cowboys either. Since Jim Crow discriminatory policies and sentiments were prevalent in the southern states, as well as other rural parts of the country, it was not uncommon for Myrtis Dightman to encounter signage prior to entering the rodeo venue that read: "no dogs, no Negroes, no Mexicans" (Wallace, 2018, p. 70). This was in spite of the Civil Rights Act of 1964. It was quite evident that he was not welcomed. If he were so fortunate to ride in mainstream rodeos, it was often after the rodeo had concluded and when the spectators left the arena. He not only draw some of the meanest bulls that had never been ridden, some stock contractors refused to permit him to ride their bulls for several reasons: (1) they could not conceive of a black rodeo cowboy riding their prized animal, and (2) they were of the opinion if, by chance, Dightman rode the bull it would bring down the animal's value and drawing ability. To assure the latter, Dightman learned probably from other black bull riders of the day to hold his free hand farther away from his body to avoid being disqualified by a racist judge. He, like Willie Thomas in a 2009 interview with the author, attempted to ride each bull well after eight seconds to assure the judges that his ride was good.

Myrtis Dightman, like Willie Thomas who is said to have put him on his first bull and James Francis who financed his career during the early years, has been an inspiration to numerous rodeo cowboys black and white whether they acknowledge it or not. His crusade to open up doors in professional rodeo paid off through his perseverance, defiance, and fearless riding, albeit oftentimes in the slack competition primarily reserved for black cowboys at mainstream rodeos. Due to spectator pressure, by infuriated fans who read in their local paper the day after the rodeo that Dightman rode an unridden bull during the evening slack competition after the fans had left the arena, the practice of forcing black cowboys to ride in slack competitions before or after the main rodeo was abandoned by the RCA. The new policy required two or three white cowboys to ride in the slack competition along with blacks. Since many white cowboys preferred to compete in front of spectators, during the main rodeo competition instead of the slack before or after the rodeo, they reluctantly opted to compete with black cowboys during the main show. In essence, Dightman subtly forced this action through his tenacious will and determination to be great. Some rodeo devotees referred to him as "the lonely bull rider" (Wallace, 2018, p. 104), an apt description of a rodeo cowboy who oftentimes had to eat, sleep, and dress in his automobile because accommodations for him on the road were either nonexistent or spartan at best. At times, he was uncertain as to whether rodeo officials would even allow him to ride. When Dightman was permitted to ride he found it most difficult to place first. Many contend it was not due to his skill level or the bulls he drew, but factors that he could not control—skin color. Freckles Brown allegedly gave his bull riding friend some candid advice about how to win the world championship: "You keep riding like you do. And turn white" (Wallace, 2018, p. 104). Dightman's grit and resolve to excel, in spite of the social challenges he faced, won over a cadre of white bull riders who offered him transportation and accommodations to various rodeos. On at least one occasion, when motel accommodations were not extended to Dightman because he was black, fellow white rodeo cowboys allegedly lowered a rope to Dightman in order for him to climb up to a second floor balcony room. However, some invitations to go down the road and compete with his white counterparts were respectfully declined. One such offer was extended to a rodeo in Montgomery, Alabama, in the late 1960s. Dightman felt that it was not the best time to rodeo in Alabama during the height of the civil rights–era unrest that was erupting in many American cities both north and south. This was the decade when prominent American leaders like President John Kennedy, civil rights activists Medgar Evers, Malcolm X, and Martin Luther King, Jr., as well as presidential candidate Robert Kennedy were all assassinated. Montgomery was an epicenter and a city that had defied various federal mandates regarding segregation and discriminatory practices. Competing in such a volatile environment, during the height of the civil rights movement and struggle for social and racial justice, could have been tragic. Dightman may very well have made one of the best decisions of his rodeo career by not competing.

Myrtis Dightman will not only be remembered for his bull riding prowess, but for his inspiration and willingness to help the next generation of bull riders. Ask Charlie Sampson, who at an early age was so enamored by Dightman that he became his mentee and a lifelong friend. Their rodeo relationship was so close that Dightman became akin to a "rodeo dad" to the young bull rider. Considerable amounts of time were spent with his mentor on the road and in Texas honing his rodeo skills. Over time he learned more than bull riding from his mentor. Sampson eventually learned patience, persistence, and the mental toughness necessary to address the uniqueness of being black riding bulls. It ultimately paid off in 1982 when Charlie Sampson won the PRCA Bull Riding World Championship. On that momentous occasion Dightman was there to assist Sampson in the chute en route to PRCA history as the first African American bull riding champion.

Whether it was to Sampson or other aspiring rodeo cowboys, Dightman has always been inspirational and would often say, "just ride." During a brief respite at the Community Faith Church in Houston, TX, with his Prairie View Trail Riders Association group in 2018, a celebratory program was staged to honor the trail riders prior to the Houston Livestock Show & Rodeo (HLS&R) Annual Parade. Dightman and his contingent are traditionally among the first to travel down the parade route. However, during the previous night's celebration Dightman was asked why he thought he could ride bulls. He nonchalantly stated: "If whites could ride why couldn't blacks, bulls don't know white from black, they just want you off their back" (Dightman, 2018). To Dightman's credit, he was the first black cowboy to ride in the Houston Astrodome where he placed first in the opening go-round of the bull riding event. He was also a multiyear National Finals Rodeo contestant from 1966 to 1972. Notwithstanding, Dightman appeared in several Hollywood movies depicting

Figure 5.5 Myrtis Dightman, the Jackie Robinson of Bull Riding with His Statue, Crockett, TX, 2016. *Source:* Courtesy of Andrea Robbins & Max Becher © 2016.

rodeo life in 1972 with legendary film icon Steve McQueen (*Junior Bonner*) and Cliff Robertson (*J. W. Coop*), who starred and directed the latter film. Dightman, shown standing with his statue (Figure 5.5), was also cast as the black Marlboro Man in cigarette commercials. It stands to reason why he is a fixture in every bull riding hall of fame. The aforementioned mid-twentieth-century black rodeo cowboys opened the door for those who would eventually follow them into rodeo arenas throughout Texas and around the country.

FOLLOWING IN THEIR FOOTSTEPS

Although the complexion of professional sport had changed considerably both literally and figuratively in the 1960s and 1970s, the vestiges of American apartheid still restricted the opportunities of black rodeo cowboys. Thus, many still "cut their teeth" and honed their skills in "all-colored" or Soul Circuit rodeos. Some of the more notable black rodeo cowboys include Taylor Hall, Jr., Freddie "Skeet" Gordon, Cleo Hearn, Paul Cleveland, Harold Cash, and Tex Williams to name a few. These individuals, in their own special way, have helped promote and maintain the Soul Circuit/ Subterranean Circuit legacy.

For example, Taylor Hall, Jr., better known to most in south Texas as "Bailey Prairie Kid," was perceived as mythical in a March 24, 2016, interview with Susan Avera Holt. The 84-year-old working cowboy, at the time of the interview, indicated that in his 70-plus years of cowboying he had worked on almost every ranch in Brazoria County. During his ranch hand days in the 1960s Bailey Prairie Kid learned how to rodeo. His versatility enabled him to compete in numerous rodeos and events for more than a decade. Highlights of his rodeo career include winning multiple championships at the Southwestern National Cowboys Association's rodeos in 1966 for saddle bronc riding, bareback bronc riding in 1968, steer wrestling in 1972 and 1973, bull riding in 1975, and as all-around champion in 1978. Bailey Prairie Kid's lifetime involvement in livestock management and outstanding rodeo career solidified his place in the Texas Rodeo Cowboy Hall of Fame with other legendary cowboys in 2001. He was also inducted into the NMWHMHF as well as the South Central Texas (SC TX) Rodeo Ring of Honor in 2019.

Soft-spoken Freddie "Skeet" Gordon has been a PRCA cardholder since 1955, and a gold card member, who still actively attends black rodeos. He is often found extolling the importance of practice and offering tips to young cowboys on the intricacies of bull riding. His 20-year multi-event rodeo career began in the mid-1950 with a first-place bull riding finish at Mercedes, TX. He frequently "went up the rode" alongside Willie Thomas and candidly spoke about the hardships black cowboys endured while competing in pre-1970 RCA events. However, in spite of the adversities, Gordon's bull riding prowess enabled him to compete in many elite rodeos from California to New York. He was a versatile rodeo cowboy who not only rode bulls but also competed in the Wild Horse Race Championship at Madison Square Garden three consecutive years (1956–1958). His specially constructed saddle gave him and his teammates a considerable advantage leading to their victories in 1957 and 1958. During those same years Gordon also rodeoed at the Boston Madison Square Garden (a.k.a. Boston Garden). His illustrious rodeo career, which included invitations to the world renown Houston Livestock Show & Rodeo (HLS&R) in the 1960s, attest to his bull riding ability. A seminal moment in Gordon's career came when he was invited to participate in the first all-African American rodeo in Harlem, NY, that included Muhammad Ali and former professional football star and actor Woody Strode. This landmark event, which occurred in 1972, was chronicled in a documentary by filmmaker Jeff Kanew and narrated by Strode. It was released shortly after the rodeo on May 1, 1972. Freddie Skeet Gordon's success in the arena has been acknowledged by several rodeo organizations. For example, the HLS&R's Black Go Texan committee inducted him into its Hall of Fame in 1995, as well as the NMWHMHF in 2011. His most recent honor came in 2019 when he was inducted into the South Central Texas (SC TX) Ring of Honor at Dripping Springs, TX.

Cleo Hern, the calf roping mentee of Marvel Rogers and founder/promoter of the Cowboys of Color Rodeo series, has been a fixture in the sport as a competitor and businessman since the late 1950s. His U2 Rodeo Productions, which has sponsored the Cowboys of Color Rodeos since 1991, is arguably the most celebrated ethnic rodeo series in the country. Advertised as the *Largest Multicultural Rodeo in the Country*, the Cowboys of Color Rodeo series combines American western frontier education and entertainment. Each rodeo incorporates culturally relevant historical facts and informational aspects pertaining to the American West: its inhabitants, rodeo events, as well as the competitions. Portions of the rodeo proceeds are earmarked for local nonprofit philanthropic causes (e.g., academic scholarships, museums, charities, etc.). He is known to some in rodeo circles as "Mr. Black Rodeo," according to Kathryn Jones, in a 2003 *Texas Journey* magazine article titled "Rodeo Renegade." To his credit Cleo Hearn was the first African American to earn a college scholarship in rodeo at Oklahoma State, first to compete in an Army rodeo, and likewise the first to win a calf roping event at a major rodeo competition: Denver National Western Stock Show (1970). He was a member of the legendary Southwest Colored Cowboys Association, and in 1971 helped establish the American Black Cowboy Association. During that same year Hearn promoted his first rodeo in Harlem, NY for 10,000 kids. This was the legendary rodeo immortalized in Jeff Kanew's documentary titled *Black Rodeo,* narrated by football star turned actor Woody Strode, featuring Muhammad Ali and a cast of African American rodeo cowboys primarily from southeast Texas.

Over the years he has maintained an active membership in numerous rodeo associations, including the PRCA since 1959, and has been inducted into several halls of fame and museums. Hearn was also inducted into the 2005 Texas Trail of Fame, adjacent to the legendary Cowtown Coliseum, in the celebrated Fort Worth Stockyards; an honor bestowed upon individuals who have made a significant contribution to the Western way of life. The Hearns are the epitome of the consummate rodeo family as all have been actively involved in rodeo competition, as well as U2 Rodeo Productions. Although Hearn continues to oversee the enterprise, his four sons which attended college on rodeo scholarships perform many of the day to day tasks in the family business. U2 Rodeo Productions' main focus, embodied in the Cowboys of Color Rodeo series and its continuity over the years, has made it a viable educational and entertainment option. To date, the Cowboys of Color Rodeo series is not only the largest and most ethnically diverse rodeo of its kind in the world, but is arguably the best.

Paul Cleveland is another Soul Circuit/Subterranean Circuit rodeo cowboy who has yet to receive the recognition deserving of a highly accomplished calf roper of the mid-1960s. His initial RCA success at the Houston Coliseum, known today as the Houston Hobby Center, was a third-place finish in the tie-down calf roping event. This was the prelude to his success at the Houston Livestock Show & Rodeo (HLS&R), which was in its first year at the Houston Astrodome. Cleveland and his personally trained horse named Stardust won first place in the Paint Horse calf-roping event in 1966. According to Cleveland's NMWHMHF induction ceremony (NMWHMHF, 2008), they returned in 1967 and won second place. This time, however, Stardust was recognized as the Best Judged Roping Horse. Like others, of his generation, after his rodeoing days came to an end Cleveland began to train horses and produce his own rodeos during the 1970s and 1980s. This enabled him to mentor young calf ropers which enabled them to hone their skills under his expert tutelage. Paul Cleveland's trained horses went on to win numerous honors at the HLS&R's Astro Arena and the Will Rogers Coliseum in Fort Worth, TX.

Another black cowboy whose rodeo career began during the celebrated years of the Soul Circuit/Subterranean Circuit was Harold Cash. A protégé of the great bull rider Willie Thomas, Cash opted to compete in the bare back riding event. He honed his skills at the S. P. Picnic Ground in Kendleton, TX, formerly a black township within the Houston-Sugar Land-Baytown metropolitan area, and the site of countless black rodeos over the years. After his disastrous first bare back ride in 1967 he eventually teamed up with Thomas, who took him under his wing in 1969 and became his longtime mentor. After several years of futility Cash began to master the nuances of professional bare back riding. Noted for riding bucking horses referred to as "Bad Ones" in his NMWHMHF induction ceremony bio-sketch, Harold Cash lived up to the "hype" when he rode a horse named Playboy in Washington, D.C.'s RFK Stadium in 1980. This was his most memorable ride because not only had Playboy never been ridden for eight seconds, but also he was touted as the "Horse of the Year." Cash went on to win the All-American Rodeo Association Bare Back title in 1979 and 1981; an organization he helped establish.

After numerous bare back riding successes Harold Cash punctuated his rodeo career with a win at the Old Time Rodeo Association bare back riding competition in 1995. As a college graduate, who used much of his rodeo winnings to help cover his tuition and fees, Cash has been keenly aware of the challenges faced by aspiring students. As a result, he annually promotes *The Harold Cash Living Legend Rodeo* to fund scholarships for underprivileged students vying for college. He also coordinates a headstone project that funds gravesite headstones for deceased black rodeo cowboys whose families are not capable of providing this tribute. Several organizations have recognized his rodeo achievements and community service. Harold Cash was inducted into The Living Legend Hall of Fame by the Black Go Texan Committee of the Houston Livestock Show and Rodeo (currently known as Black Heritage Committee) in 2003 and the NMWHMHF in 2010.

Equally skilled yet rarely mentioned among southeast Texas rodeo legends is Tex Williams, whose prospective rodeo career was "short circuited" when he was drafted into the military to serve in the Vietnam War. Born on a ranch in the Blue Creek area of El Campo, TX, Williams started rodeoing at an early age riding the family cow at 12 years old. Due in part to his early exposure to ranch life, Williams honed his rodeo skills well beyond his age. He became the first African American schoolboy to compete in the Texas High School Rodeo Championship in 1967, shortly after high school rodeos were desegregated, and subsequently won the All-Around Championship. He duplicated the feat at the state rodeo championship in 1968. Tex Williams also made history when he became the first African American to compete in the National High School Rodeo Finals in 1967. Williams was so adept at rodeoing as a youth he often competed against some of the best professional rodeo cowboys of the day, most of which participated in Soul Circuit/Subterranean Circuit competitions due to segregation. His rodeoing took him to South Texas Junior College where he made the National Intercollegiate Rodeo Association (NIRA) finals in 1969 at Deadwood, SD. Upon returning from active military service, Williams was unwilling to subject himself to the many indignities still rampant in American society and the sport of rodeo in the 1970s. Thus, he opted to forgo the sport on a full-time basis. Williams has yet to hang up his spurs and competes periodically on the senior circuit. In 1998, riding rough stock, he won All-Around Cowboy in the Old Timer Rodeo Association. More recently he made the World Series in Team Roping and placed fifth in Las Vegas in 2017. Due to his many accomplishments, Williams has been nominated to several national and state halls of fame. His numerous belt buckles and saddles won in the rodeo arena makes a strong case for the schoolboy sensation from El Campo.

Several non-Texans who picked up where black rodeo cowboys of the 1970s left off and found mentorship riding the Soul Circuit/Subterranean Circuit were Sylvester Mayfield of Clovis, NM, and Charles Sampson of Los Angeles, CA. Each became successful in their respective events at elite PRCA competitions. Mayfield was a two-time NFR qualifier (1985 and 1987) in the tie-down roping competition and won the event at the Calgary Stampede (1985) and Fort Worth Stock Show (1987). Since retirement, Mayfield has become a successful cattle rancher and horse trainer. The Mayfield rodeo tradition is currently maintained by his son Shad, a tie-down roper like his dad, and daughter Shelby who is a barrel racer on her Eastern New Mexico rodeo team. Both have aspirations of competing in the NFR one day. Charles "Charlie" Sampson, the diminutive 5' 4" 134-pound bull rider, a.k.a. "Pee Wee" and "Mighty Mite" was a Dightman protégé who learned his lessons well. Sampson aspired to ride bulls ever since the day he saw Myrtis Dightman traveling through town and hanging out at the El Fig Stables in 1972. Sampson was so impressed with the traveling black rodeo cowboy that he wanted to be just like him. He eventually found the courage to meet Dightman and mentioned his desire to emulate him and travel the world rodeoing. Dightman apparently saw something in Sampson and agreed to mentor him provided that he finish high school.

The mentee did, while riding bulls, and eventually enrolled at Central Arizona College on a rodeo scholarship. Sampson competed on the college rodeo circuit for several years but yearned for the big time. In 1977 he joined the PRCA and was one of only a handful of black cowboys competing. Shortly thereafter Sampson relocated to Crockett, TX, in 1978 to train with his idol Myrtis Dightman, who had begun to wind down his bull riding career. The aged bull rider and his mentee began traveling to rodeos together. Christian Wallace captured Sampson's perspective of this dubious pairing in a 2018 interview for Texas Monthly. He stated, "… I really got a taste of what it was like to travel with greatness. Here I was, living out a lifelong dream, following in Myrtis's footsteps" (p. 106). Sampson was always in awe of his mentor, and as a result the young bull rider's avidity and desire to excel in the sport escalated immeasurably. Even during the tough times when injuries short circuited his success and biased judging appeared to be a predominant factor Sampson was able to lean on his mentor for inspiration. Having experienced the latter more times than he will admit, Dightman implored his protégé to just ride. He knew that there were individuals in the sport who were not receptive to black cowboys and realized that you cannot ride and judge too. Success eventually came to Sampson.

In 1981 a healthy Charlie Sampson qualified for the NFR, the first time a black cowboy had done so since Dightman in 1972. The next year Sampson not only qualified for the NFR but won the world championship, a feat never accomplished by a black cowboy. During his illustrious 17-year rodeo career Sampson qualified for the NFR ten times and won numerous elite PRCA competitions in the United States and Canada. Throughout the 1980s he was one of the highest money-winning bull riders and set a record for monetary winnings in 1982. A major draw during the height of his career, Sampson was voted the "Coors Fan Favorite Cowboy" in 1986. Although he retired in 1994, his bull riding success, product endorsements, and celebrity appearances have enabled him to earn more than a million dollars. He is a fixture in every recognized rodeo hall of fame in the country: ProRodeo Hall of

Fame (1996), NMWHMHF (2003), Rodeo Hall of Fame of the National Cowboy and Western Heritage Museum (2008), Ellensburg Rodeo Hall of Fame (2009), and Bull Riding Hall of Fame (2019). However, Sampson still enjoys instructing novice bull riders and spending time with various youth groups. Among his favorite are the Boys and Girls Clubs and the Boy Scouts of America. The latter is where he got his passion for horses.

Like many of the elite black rodeo cowboys that preceded them, unfortunately, few were able to compete full time on the circuit due to domestic obligations that necessitated full-time employment. Thus, they competed when they could, even during times when they were in the midst of their employment obligations. Not only were these stellar black rodeo cowboys unable to compete nationally like their white counterparts, but the black rodeo prize money was rarely enough to enable them to travel to the more distant and lucrative rodeos. When they did go down the road their mode of travel, restaurant arrangements, and lodging accommodations were often spartan at best. A strategic plan of action had to be created when black rodeo cowboys traveled outside of their normal environs because all hotels/motels, eateries, and service stations did not readily accept their patronage, particularly in many small rural towns. Therefore, the use of the legendary *"Green Book"* a.k.a. *"The Negro Motorist Green Book"* served as a contemporary travel guide and/or GPS for locating establishments that would provide basic amenities to African Americans. The travel hardships experienced throughout the country by black rodeo cowboys prior to federal mandates prohibited many from competing in some of the more distant lucrative rodeos. According to previous research published in *The Journal of American Culture* (2004), most black rodeo cowboys primarily competed in the smaller "open" rodeos within a 200–250-mile radius of their hometowns while attempting to compete in multiple rodeos concurrently. Several federal laws passed in the 1960s (e.g., Civil Rights Act of 1964 and 1968) and the expansion of the interstate highway system provided a modicum of support for black rodeo cowboys who took to the rode, but in various parts of rural America very little had changed. Jim Crow laws and discriminatory practices remained the norm.

ANCILLARY COMPONENTS BUT ESSENTIAL

Over the years there have been numerous individuals and organizations that served in an ancillary capacity to facilitate and maintain the legacy of the Soul Circuit/Subterranean Circuit in the Texas Gulf Coast region, as well as the black cowboys who rode it. These stakeholders were instrumental in myriad ways. Without the financial support and patronage of this collective entity this sociocultural phenomenon would not have occurred. Included are arena owners, veterinarians, rodeo promoters, announcers, sponsors, stock contractors, entertainers, and concessionaires to name a few. These individuals are referred to as such only because they serve in a "support" capacity for the rodeo and its participants. They were, and are, undeniably essential components in the rodeo production.

Their involvement during the pre-integration Jim Crow era was more critical than ever because black rodeo cowboys had limited participation opportunities within mainstream rodeo. Thus, the black rodeo was often the only option available. Much like Negro League Baseball black rodeos provided "safe spaces," communal meeting sites, an entertainment option free of the restrictions imposed in mainstream society, and a minor economic windfall for concessionaires, as well as local merchants within the vicinity. For example, many rodeos, including the Houston Livestock Show and Rodeo had restrictions on when blacks could attend and where they were permitted to sit in the arena. An interview with a longtime Soul Circuit/Subterranean Circuit rodeo announcer in 2004 confirmed the discriminatory treatment at a fairground in Center, TX. He stated that they didn't let blacks in the fairground, and that a white man at the gate said, "Negroes night was on Tuesday" (personal communication, A. F., September 2, 2004). A. F. was accompanied by the legendary bull rider Willie Thomas, who requested that the gatekeeper call the "head man" in Denver, CO, for access to the rodeo arena. He did, and the head man responded insisting that they let Thomas ride. He rode after the crowd had left the arena, in what is commonly referred to as the slack competition, and won the bull riding event. It is important to note that prior to integration the slack competition was mainly the time set aside before and after the main show, and spectators left, when black cowboys were permitted to compete. The contemporary slack competition is valued by rodeo cowboys white and black alike because it affords them the opportunity to compete in multiple rodeos concurrently.

Several of the notable stakeholders responsible for the Soul Circuit's longevity through the years were James Francies, a trail riding friend of Myrtis Dightman from Prairie View (TX), who helped Dightman establish the Prairie View Trail Riders Association in 1957. He also financially sponsored him during his early rodeo career. Alfred Poindexter, a longtime veterinary professor at Prairie View A&M University and cofounder of the aforementioned trail riding association, tended to many of the animals involved in the rodeo competitions. Mark Hatfield and Troy John (a.k.a. T. J.) Williams were renown horse trainers and mentors to many aspiring rodeo cowboys seeking help in preparing their horses for competitions. T. J. was known by many as the "Tennis Shoe Cowboy" because he trained horses in athletic shoes primarily due to a calf roper's horrific injury he witnessed. His extraordinary ability to train cutting horses for Soul Circuit/Subterranean Circuit and PRCA cowboys gave him a marketable reputation throughout Texas. He developed the Live Oak training center, which was a premiere facility for black rodeo cowboys and casual riders alike.

A. J. Walker (Circle 6 Ranch) and Robert Jackson (R. V. Ranch) were rodeo cowboys who also promoted rodeo competitions at their respective ranches dating back to the mid-1950s. Walker helped establish the ASGCA to help hone the rodeo skills of black cowboys and provide rodeo opportunities for them in southeast Texas. Jackson did similar things in the quaint rural community of McBeth, TX. He was a member of the Southwestern National Cowboys Association (SNCA) and served as its president and treasurer over the years. Jackson and SNCA established arenas in Houston, Dickenson, Egypt, Kendleton, Jones Creek, and McBeth where he also competed in several events (calf roping, team roping, steer wrestling, and breakaway roping). The R.V. Ranch rodeo promotion legacy, similar to that of the Hearn's but at a much smaller level, continues under the stewardship of one of Jackson's sons, Ramone.

Although many of those who promoted black rodeos at their respective ranches may have provided their own rough stock for the competitions; however, one name most often mentioned with regard to stock contracting is Melvin Glover. Known as the stock contractor with one arm, due to a ranch related injury, Glover has promoted and provided the stock for some of the largest black rodeos in Texas. His annual Madisonville rodeo which was always well attended relocated to the Robertson County Fairgrounds at Hearn, TX, in 2002, a short drive down the road from Texas A&M University's main campus in College Station (TX). Hotel and motel accommodations for this event must be booked well in advance and travel routes scrutinized specifically to navigate the congested highways during this annual rodeo scheduled for the third week in September. The Glover Legacy Rodeos have been so successful, and a community staple, that the Madisonville rodeo was resurrected in 2008 under the leadership of Glover's daughter, Melva Glover. Because of its notoriety, finding a viable venue to accommodate the many spectators and rodeo contestants has been a challenge. Since 2011 it has been held at the Madison County Fairgrounds Arena. To date, Melvin Glover has been among the most successful stock contractors and promotors of black rodeos since the 1980s. Although semi-retired as the prominent promotor of the Glover Legacy Rodeos, he is usually on site and available even when he is not working the event.

An often-neglected ancillary component, yet vital to the success of each and every rodeo, is the bull fighter. Known to most naïve rodeo spectators as the rodeo clown, these courageous individuals and their unique skills oftentimes save bull riders from major animal inflicted injuries. According to a rodeo risk factor study conducted by my colleague and I and published in 1999, their job is arguably the most dangerous in the sport because of the incidence of injury. One of the most celebrated bull fighters in the history of rodeo is Luke "Leon" Coffey. He was the first black bullfighter to be selected to work the National Finals Rodeo (NFR) during his rookie year in 1979. A "want-to-be" rodeo cowboy at an early age in Blanco, TX, Coffey competed in Little Britches contests, the Texas Youth Rodeo Association, and qualified for the National High School Rodeo Finals as a bareback rider. However, he not only competed in rodeo competitions, but was a Texas All-State linebacker and brown belt recipient in karate. Billed as the "Boogie Man" and "The Disco Cowboy" partly due to his bull inducing dances choreographed many years ago, Coffey is known as much for his crowd entertaining comedic routines as his cowboy saving maneuvers. He is also fondly referred to as the "Man in the Can" because of his legendary barrel antics. Coffey's signature green cowboy hat, multicolored shirt, baggie jeans, and painted face, have made him quite possibly the most revered and beloved rodeo clown in the sport's history.

Leon Coffey was a multiyear NFR selected bullfighter/clown/barrel man and a Lifetime Gold Card PRCA member. His career, which spanned over 30 years, and the multiple fractures and broken bones incurred in the arena attest to his longevity in this injury susceptible rodeo activity. Coffey's legendary accomplishments have not gone unnoticed. He was inducted into the Texas Rodeo Cowboy Hall of Fame (2004), NMWHMHF (2005), Pro Rodeo Hall of Fame (2018), and Texas Bull Riding Hall of Fame (2019). A longtime crowd favorite, Coffey still participates in charity events and visits the children's wards at local hospitals. Very few have galvanized rodeo audiences as Leon Coffey has during his four-decade rodeo career.

Other support staff instrumental in the rodeo production and its marketing, which invariably impacts spectator satisfaction, gate receipts, and rodeo cowboy payouts are the show announcers and musical entertainers. The legendary voices of announcers Hadley Barrett and Bob Tallman were behind their respective microphones for PRCA rodeos for more than five decades. Their fan-friendly approach have made them PRCA Hall of Fame inductees and basically irreplaceable. Although not nationally renowned as Hadley and Tallman, early Soul Circuit/Subterranean Circuit rodeo announcers of the 1940s and 1950s like Jim Smith, Jonah Warren, and Preacher Williams were the pioneers. They passed the microphone like a baton in the 1960s to Lorenzo "Smitty" Johnson and Jim Richard, Jr., who would become the most celebrated announcers of black rodeo for nearly 50 years. Richards announced his last rodeo in 2009 while Johnson's was a year later. The latter was noted for announcing Black Heritage Night at the Houston Livestock Show & Rodeo (HLSR) with Bob Tallman. It was the most anticipated day of events and activities for African Americans at the HLSR, as it celebrated the contributions of black cowboys in shaping Western culture. Smitty Johnson was a crowd favorite announcer who revised the Cowboy Prayer and salute to Old Glory recited before most every black rodeo. He was so good at his craft spectators were known to arrive early and line up outside the arena in order to get a good seat just to hear his rendition of the Cowboy Prayer and salute to Old Glory.

Two of the more contemporary voices that followed Johnson and Richards at select black rodeos in the new millennium were Dwight "Hollywood" Davis and Tony Parker. Hollywood, the more thespian-like of the two, has been a fan favorite primarily because he announces and informs the audience of the nuances of each event while entertaining them with puns and comedic phrases simultaneously. Unlike many of his peers, Hollywood literally prefers to be close to the action. Oftentimes he announces the rodeo in the arena, on the dirt, and astride his well-trained steed. His deference and support of the competing rodeo cowboy regardless of what happens in the arena conveys a special message to fans and cowboys alike.

Musical entertainment has been a staple at rodeos for much of the twentieth century. Reminiscent of cowboys sitting around a prairie campfire after a long day of herding, musical entertainment has been a major marketing ploy and of late may rival the rodeo itself as the core product. Historically, the HLSR has served as a major purveyor of musical entertainment when it initiated this component with "The Singing Cowboy" Gene Autry in 1942. Due to its enormous success HLSR has continued to employ this strategy well into the new millennium with an annual star-studded lineup of the most sought after musical entertainers in the country. Not only have major mainstream rodeos used musical entertainment to increase attendance and fan satisfaction, Soul Circuit/Subterranean Circuit rodeos have done likewise. Although their budgets have not afforded them the ability to attract the top musical entertainers, it has enabled local musicians like Larry Callies to "cut their teeth" on the circuit and achieve a modicum amount of national notoriety. Callies became a regular performer, with his Bronco Band, at the annual Simonton Rodeo (TX). As a generational rodeo cowboy, whose dad was a successful calf roper and veteran ranch hand for legendary stock contractor Sloan Williams, Callies learned ranching and rodeoing at a very young age and has numerous belt buckles to validate his success. Among Callies' proudest moments was being the second black teen to qualify for the Texas High School Rodeo State Finals in 1971. Ironically his cousin Tex Williams was the first in 1967.

In 1985 Callies traded his chaps, spurs, and calf roping tack for a guitar, which launched a successful singing career. Noted for being the opening act for country music stars Collin Raye and two-time Grammy award winner Travis Tritt, as well as Tejano legends Emilio Navaira, dubbed the "Garth Brooks of Tejano," and Salena Quintanilla, known as the "Queen of Tejano" music, Callies has been a feature entertainer at numerous black rodeos during his 35-year singing career. Singing on a part-time basis due to a voice disorder known as vocal dysphonia, Callies is currently the curator/owner of *The Black Cowboy Museum* and a saddlery business located in Richmond (TX) not far from the legendary George Ranch where he worked for several years.

Although the musical genre and delivery system have varied greatly over the years, particularly within black rodeos, music is still without question instrumental in the marketing of successful contemporary rodeos. An added feature in many black rodeos over the years has been the post-rodeo dance, which at times is held in the arena on the dirt. On these occasions spectators and rodeo cowboys mix and mingle in what has been marketed as "KICK'IN THE DIRT."

REFERENCES

Allen, M. (1998). *Rodeo Cowboys in the North American Imagination*. Reno, NV: University of Nevada Press.

Angelle, D. (1989, February 26). Grandfathers proud of their early rodeo days. *Houston Chronicle*, p. C2 West.

Carrizales, O. (2013). Green, Rufus, Sr. *Handbook of Texas Online*, Texas State Historical Association. Retrieved from http://www.tshaonline.org/handbook/online/articles/fgrca

Coakley, J. (2009). *Sport in Society: Issues and Controversies* (10th ed.). Boston, MA: McGraw-Hill.

Dightman, M. (2018, February 22). Rodeo and trail rider exhibit, *Community Faith Church*. Houston, TX.

Farrell, J. (2019, January 17). 1st Annual George Ranch Rodeo to Honor Black Cowboy Legacy of Fort Bend County. *George Ranch Media Release*. Retrieved from https://www.georgeranch.org/news/1st-annual-george-ranch-rodeo-to-honor-black-cowboy-legacy-of-fort-bend-county/

Haney, C. A., & Pearson, D. W. (1999). Rodeo injuries: An examination of risk factors. *Journal of Sport Behavior, 22*(4), 443–466.

Hobbs, F., & Stoops, N. (2002). *Demographic Trends in the 20th Century: Census 2000 Special Reports*. U.S. Census Bureau. Washington, D.C.: U.S. Government Printing Office.

Jackson, E., Jr. (2000). *Celebrating Black Cowboys in 2000* [Brochure]. Houston, TX: Clear Channel Communications.

Jones, K. (July/August, 2003). Rodeo renegade. *Texas Journey*, 68.

Katz, L. W. (1996). *The Black West*. New York, NY: Simon & Schuster.

Lawson, M. W. (1983). *Calf Roping with Rufus Green: Fact or Fiction*. Austin, TX: Eakin Press, 1983.

Lioznyansky, V. (Producer & Director). (2013). *African-American Cowboy – The Forgotten Man of the West* [Documentary film]. United States: https://www.youtube.com/watch?v=5jwlMtg4ts8

Manley, E., & Hardwick, L. H. (1976). *Negro Baseball . . . Before Integration*. Haworth, NJ: St. Johann Press.

O'Hara, S. J. P., & Service, A. (2018, July 19). Champions of the rodeo. *North Coast Journal*. Retrieved from https://www.northcoastjournal.com/humboldt/champions-of-the-rodeo/Content?oid=10085177

Patton, T. O., & Schedlock, S. M. (2011). Let's go, let's show, let's rodeo: African Americans and the history of rodeo. *The Journal of African American History, 96*(4), 503–521.

Pearson, D. W. (2004). Shadow riders of the subterranean circuit: A descriptive account of Black rodeo in the Texas Gulf Coast region. *The Journal of American Culture, 27*(2), 190–198.

Pearson, D W. (2009). Black in the saddle: The best bull rider you never saw. In J. L. Conyers, Jr. (Ed.), *Racial Structure & Radical Politics in the African Diaspora, Africana Studies* (Vol. 3, pp. 183–196). New Brunswick, NJ: Transaction.

Pearson, D. W., & Haney, C. A. (1999). The rodeo cowboy: Cultural icon, athlete or entrepreneur? *Journal of Sport and Social Issues, 23*(3), 308–327.

SC TX Rodeo. (2019, October). *5th Annual SCTX Rodeo Ring of Honor Cowboy Reunion*. South Central Texas Rodeo Connection, Dripping Springs Ranch Park, Dripping Springs, TX. http://www.sctxrodeo.com/index.html

Wallace, C. (2018, January). The greatest. *Texas Monthly*, pp. 66–71, 98–107.

Wallach, D. (2016, July 5). Jefferson county rancher, cowboy rides into western heritage hall of fame. *Beaumont Enterprise*. Retrieved from https://www.beaumontenterprise.com/news/texas/article/Jefferson-County-rancher-cowboy-rides-in-to-8341127.php

Watriss, W. (1980, December). The soul circuit. *Geo, 2*, 134–150.

Weston, J. (1985). *The Real American Cowboy*. New York, NY: Schocken Books.

Chapter 6

Shadow Riders of the Subterranean Circuit

[1]African Americans have experienced unparalleled racial intolerance and discrimination in every conceivable form since their arrival in New World over 400 years ago. This form of disenfranchisement has operated in all aspects of society, including work and play. North American rodeo, whose origins can be traced to festival pastimes in Mexico and its cattle industry, evolved into a quasi-sport form in the United States during the late nineteenth century (Pearson & Haney, 1999a). This work-related sport form incorporated the social and cultural controls endemic to American society. As a result, even though blacks were inextricably involved in the cattle industry, rodeo, and "the West," American history has frequently misrepresented, marginalized, or omitted their contributions. However, some researchers (Newman, 1997) have argued that the term "cowboy" may have first been used to denote a black slave's role in the cattle industry in east coast plantations and farms.

Rodeo, like baseball and other American sports, was participated in and influenced by African American athletes whose legacy within the sport has also been frequently overlooked. Interestingly, unbeknownst to many, a rodeo circuit exists in Texas comprised primarily of African American rodeo cowboys. The participants, past and present, have received minimal media exposure as well as the venues housing their sport. Yet, they continue to compete and maintain the cultural trappings of the past.

This serendipitous rodeo circuit offers a unique opportunity to analyze the nuances of ethnic rodeo, in a novel environment to most scholars. Staged in small rural environs, this branch of rodeo reflects sanctioned mainstream rodeo, yet departs from it in several respects. Veteran cowboys and observers have dubbed it the "Soul Circuit" (Watriss, 1980). I have referred to it in my work as the "Subterranean Circuit" because of several unique features: it is rarely reported in the media, few are aware of its history and existence, arenas are located in obscure locales, and attendance is comprised of the devotees. Also, the rodeo cowboys have been referred to as "Shadow Riders" because they have historically participated in rodeo competitions in the shadows of their white counterparts. Unfortunately, often barred from competing in mainstream rodeos while spectators were present, black cowboys were forced to ride before and/or after the show in what has been called the slack competition. The Soul Circuit or Subterranean Circuit is a loosely structured network of ethnic rodeos that have operated in the Gulf Coast region of Texas since the 1940s. This area is unique in that it has the largest number of African American rodeo cowboys in the world (Watriss, 1980), as does the state of Texas with respect to rodeo cowboys in general.

RODEO AND AMERICANA: A BRIEF HISTORICAL REVIEW

American rodeo has recently experienced a resurgence in popularity since its dramatic decline in the late 1950s. Akin to the Hollywood-produced western, rodeo may have fallen victim to a more radical social and political climate in the 1960s. Today, more than 43 million people identify themselves as fans of professional rodeo (PRORODEO, 2020). This figure currently ranks rodeo seventh in overall attendance among major sporting events, ahead of golf and tennis. Rodeo fans can now follow the sport year-round through various mediums including Professional Rodeo Cowboys Association (PRCA)'s television coverage on CBS Sports Network, its ProRodeo Sports News magazine, ProRodeo.com, and sundry rodeo-related outlets. The aforementioned figure does not include the countless unsanctioned professional rodeos held in small rural towns around the country. Evidence of rodeo's resurgence has also been demonstrated by network viewership. The Nashville Network televises Professional Bull Riders (PBR) and PRCA competitions to millions of fans weekly. Additionally, the PRCA has recently launched The Cowboy Channel Plus App which can be streamed on any device, allowing fans fingertip access to rodeos throughout the day. Surprisingly, over 20 years ago the PRCA's Media Guide indicated that more than 15 million viewers watched professional rodeo on television in 1998 (PRCA, 1999). Considering the data, it is difficult to dismiss the impact of rodeo as a viable sport and entertainment option based on the demand.

Critics and sport purists alike have questioned its athletic pedigree and sport skill requirements and have characterized it as spectacle. However, contemporary rodeo incorporates the requisite elements detailed by Coakley (2001) for any sport form. In addition, rodeo rests upon rich cultural tradition and history, ritualistic lore, and fanatical bravado conceivably unparalleled in modern sports. "Perhaps no other sport in the United States, except baseball, is seen as epitomizing American values, traditions and lifestyles as does rodeo" (Pearson & Haney, 1999b, p. 17). These may have been factors contributing to the popularity and patriotic fervor imbued by rodeo during World War II when other sport forms were temporarily canceled.

Historically, rodeo parallels American culture since it was participated in and influenced by minority athletes whose legacy has been marginalized and overlooked. An example of this omission is Bill Pickett, an African American from Taylor, Texas, who is credited for having invented "bulldogging": a popular rodeo event commonly known as steer wrestling. Until he became a celebrity for his trademark bulldogging technique, Pickett was forced to dress as a Mexican toreador because rodeos did not admit black contestants. Early accounts of the ranching industry in and around Texas, Oklahoma, and the Mexican border address various cultural and festival pastimes. Rodeos were a common fixture within this region and engaged in by Anglos, as well as Hispanics, African Americans, and Native Americans (Blanchard, 1995). Although rarely depicted in film, historical evidence suggest that at least one in three cowboys was "of color" (Collins & McIngvale, 1997). As a result, an estimated 9,000 African Americans participated in the cattle industry in the late 1800s. As Lawrence noted, "It was a society of white Anglo-Saxon domination, in which Mexican and black cowboys were often discriminated against and were not generally promoted to foremen" (1982, p. 67). Often, they were hired to do the hardest and most dangerous jobs.

Unable to compete in rodeos of the day, due to unwritten policies excluding them, African Americans began to organize their own competitions and associations. Jackson (2000) conveyed this point:

> Although the Professional Rodeo Cowboys Association (PRCA) never had a written policy that excluded minority competitors, it is interesting to read comments from older cowboys . . . reference to "the days of segregated rodeo." Until around the 1950's, the lack of black professional cowboys and some underlying racism kept most blacks from competing with whites. To combat this situation, black cowboys of the 1940s formed the Southwestern Colored Cowboys Association (SCCA). (p. 12)

Although such policies based on race no longer exist, professional rodeos comprised primarily of African American cowboys still operate throughout the country. These little-known subterranean circuits continue to offer a viable sport opportunity and entertainment option. Even though more has been written in the last decade about the sport and lifestyle of the rodeo cowboy little seems to have been documented regarding African American involvement in rodeo. In many respects, these rodeo cowboys remain relatively invisible.

THE SOUL CIRCUIT SETTING

The Soul Circuit or Subterranean Circuit is located in and around the Texas Gulf Coast region. Many of the individuals interviewed and discussed are descendants of former slaves brought to Texas to labor on sugar and cotton plantations, as well as cattle ranches in Fort Bend, Brazoria, Liberty, and Jefferson counties. Others are descendants of former slaves that had migrated to the lush grasslands of the Texas Gulf Coast from Arkansas and Louisiana after the Civil War. Many were attracted to the coastal counties because of the labor demands and quest for land. Mid- to late-nineteenth-century African Americans residing in these rural environs were often employed as migrant farmers, domestics, livestock caretakers, and cowboys. As a result, black settlements (e.g., Kendleton) and towns densely populated by African Americans (i.e., Prairie View, Richmond, Egypt, etc.) emerged. Like other indigenous groups within Texas, festive pastimes that included ranch livestock became prevalent. Ro-day-os or the anglicized term "rodee-os" were staged to test various skills of the ranch hands. Since Jim Crow laws relegated African Americans to second class citizenry few blacks were permitted to participate in white promoted rodeos. As a result, African Americans staged their own competitions. Population patterns, much like today, dictated where the early rodeos were staged. Many of the early sites make up the contemporary Soul Circuit. The term Soul Circuit, fondly used by veteran performers and spectators, denotes the loosely structured schedule of minority rodeos held in and around the Texas Gulf Coast region. This area includes Houston and much smaller cities to the east (e.g., Beaumont, Raywood, and Liberty); Dallas and surrounding cities to the north (e.g., Fort Worth, Madisonville, and Fairfield); San Antonio and quaint prairie towns to the west (e.g., Navasota and Hempstead); and small, southern, rural communities like Egypt, McBeth, and Kendleton. Some of these areas are historically significant because of their tie to the cattle, agriculture, and slave industries.

SHADOW RIDERS

The rodeo cowboys that make up the Soul Circuit are part-time rodeo performers, for the most part. Many hold full-time jobs while rodeoing. This factor has a major impact on African Americans' access to the nationally sanctioned PRCA rodeos. Because of their full-time employment, limited disposable income, and lack of sponsorship few African American cowboys, contrary to their white counterparts, find it possible to leave their jobs midweek to travel to distant rodeo sites. These circumstances are akin to the plight of African American athletes in auto racing. As a result, most African American rodeo cowboys are attracted to the small, unsanctioned, open rodeos, frequently scheduled on the weekends. These rodeos are usually within a 200–250-mile radius of the rodeo cowboy's hometown.

Although many indicated that they had participated in rodeos at an early age, most had little formal training in the sport. Unlike their white counterparts who may have engaged in structured programs like 4-H Clubs, Little Britches Rodeos, and scholastic rodeo programs, few of the minority cowboys expressed such involvement; nor had many participated in weekend rodeo schools or college rodeo programs. Of those interviewed few had actually honed their skills on a working ranch. This fact was articulated by a veteran Soul Circuit cowboy and once aspiring Negro League ballplayer, who grew up on a ranch and herded cattle during the Jim Crow era. L. R. lamented:

> Ninety-nine percent of the rodeo cowboys competing in this rodeo don't know what to do on a ranch. I came up through the ranks. We used to break horses for $10.00 a head and could only practice at stock contractor breakouts. They're not as talented as we were partly due to the opportunities to do other things.

Many contemporary Soul Circuit cowboys admitted that they had learned their rodeo skills from watching television, "shadowing" veteran cowboys over the years, and trial and error in the arena. C. M., a PRCA card holder and Soul Circuit competitor, stated: "I actually got started by watching rodeo competitions on TV. I was about 12 [years old] when a cousin and his friends got me in it." He indicated that his rodeo involvement tends to be a bit different than many of his Soul Circuit counterparts:

> Since I'm employed as a rancher, I have a flexible schedule. It also helps to have a boss that's a calf roper. He competes too. My schedule is not too hectic so I can travel out of state about once a month. I don't have a major preference toward sanction or unsanctioned competitions. Where the show is, and the cost determine if I am riding.

C. M.'s experiences are somewhat unique to those of his counterparts since he has calf roped at the collegiate level, is a PRCA member, and plans part of his rodeo schedule based on PRCA information and the Cowboy Sports News. Few that ride the Soul Circuit have the aforementioned benefits. Yet, with limited formal training and ranching experience to draw upon, Soul Circuit rodeo cowboys continue to seek fame and fortune via the less heralded, small circuit, weekend rodeos, in rural Texas environs.

RODEO VENUES

Facilities reminiscent of the years of segregated baseball appear to be prevalent at Soul Circuit rodeo venues. Although the viability of some of the sites might be questioned, event promoters frequently make do with the dimly lighted, cramped, and dilapidated facilities. Worn and rusted pens, splinter infested wooden bleachers, unfinished press boxes with barely audible sound systems, makeshift concession and pay booths are part of the legacy and reality of the Circuit. Space dimensions of the rodeo arenas vary considerably depending upon ownership. Whereas fairgrounds tended to be spacious with ample competition area and seating, private ranches and local rodeo arenas often lacked extensive seating. The competition areas, albeit quaint, were large enough for the requisite events. The event most apt to be compromised was barrel racing due to its space requirements for the start-up and deceleration phases.

Parking at many Soul Circuit rodeos was not of major concern, particularly in comparison to densely populated urban sites. The rural environment where many of these venues were located afforded certain amenities. At some venues it was common practice for spectators to back their pick-up trucks to the arena fence and view the rodeo from the truck's bed. The more contemporary rodeo arenas or fairgrounds often had standard parking lots. Regardless of the venue, parking fees were modest ranging from $1.00 to $3.00. Several venues either had no parking fee or the cost was included in the ticket price. A major shortcoming at some of the smaller venues was the portable restrooms, which were "Spartan" at best. These facilities were less than ideal, particularly at rodeos scheduled in the evening.

Spectator amenities varied depending upon the respective venue. Generally, rodeos held at fairgrounds, offered a more comfortable environment. Frequently county-owned and operated, these facilities were often covered and equipped with indoor restrooms. Lighting, parking, and signage were standard; while concession windows and stands were easily accessible. Since the rentals of such facilities were more costly than smaller local sites, promoters frequently made concerted efforts to solicit sponsors to defray operating cost. Thus, advertising banners and placards were frequently draped across and affixed to arena rails and fencing.

Concession stands and food windows are major revenue sources at all sport and entertainment venues, and Soul Circuit rodeos were no exception. Assorted items were available to be purchased including Western attire, riding gear, jewelry, beverages, and food. Akin to mainstream rodeos that highlight barbecue flavored meats, Soul Circuit "cuisine" also featured fried catfish and boudain (Cajun sausage). Both foods are culturally significant and indigenous to the devotees, as well as fan favorites and dietary staples. These delectables could be purchased outside the arena prior to the rodeo at various contracted food trucks that paid for space or inside the arena at the indoor concession stand.

MARKETING AND PROMOTIONAL STRATEGIES

The marketing and promotional strategies employed over the years in the Soul Circuit/Subterranean Circuit were provincial and lacking contemporary technological advances. Unlike many mainstream rodeo circuits which utilized audio-visual, print, and electronic medias to market and promote events, the Soul Circuit/Subterranean Circuit primarily depended on handbills, such as the one shown (Figure 6.1), posters, public address announcements (at rodeos), and word of mouth. The absence of the more sophisticated forms of advertising appeared to be due in part to limited revenue streams, the lack of corporate sponsors, nominal promotional budgets, and spectator resources (e.g., computers). Thus, the promotional activities primarily attracted local cowboys and rodeo fans from around the general area.

The Cowboys of Color rodeos, which consisted of a series of individual rodeo competitions co-sponsored by Ford and held in five Texas cities (i.e., San Antonio, Austin, Houston, Fort Worth, and Mesquite) in 2001, were the only minority-oriented rodeos which utilized contemporary technological advances to advertise. The promoter (C. H.) of this invitational rodeo series was adamant about the importance of implementing new promotional strategies with conventional techniques. Billboards, websites, radio and television spots, handbills, calendars, souvenir programs and apparel were employed for promotional purposes. He contended that ethnic rodeos can be successful endeavors if they attract corporate sponsors that can help sell their product. According to C. H.,

> Anything that Blacks are candidates to buy can help underwrite cost and promote the rodeo. Tobacco, beer, banking, food, electronics, news services, utility companies and small businesses [e.g., legal and tax services, funeral homes, and feed stores] are potential sponsors. The important thing is, you have to sell them on a quality rodeo. No one wants to be associated with a bad product.

The Cowboys of Color invitational rodeos have been very successful in attracting corporate sponsorship, which in turn has enhanced the image of the rodeo, provided multiple advertising outlets, more participants, and increased winning payouts. This rodeo series was most like mainstream rodeos with respect to marketing and promotion, yet maintained the trappings of ethnic rodeos (e.g., food, music, specialty events, and post-rodeo entertainment).

Figure 6.1 Rodeo Handbill: Trailride and Rodeo.

Among the more noteworthy marketing and promotional ploys implemented by Soul Circuit/Subterranean Circuit promoters were the post-rodeo dances and specialty events. The rodeo dance is a staple and major component within black rodeo. With live entertainment, frequently featuring Zydeco music (a combination of Cajun, Rhythm and Blues, and Country and Western), the rodeo dance provides additional value to the cost of admission. In many of the small, rural locales in Texas, the rodeo and dance compete favorably with high school football for the entertainment dollar. However, due to the need to maximize the potential spectator base many rodeos were scheduled for Saturday evenings and Sunday afternoons so as not to conflict with football during the fall months.

To further attract a paying audience, ethnic rodeo promoters have often included specialty events. These events frequently include roughstock and timed roping competitions for young children (i.e., "Pee Wees" and "Juniors") and older adults ("Old Timers"). The specialty events served multiple purposes: rodeo socialization for the youth, a feeder system program for the rodeo circuit, inclusion for young and old rodeo contestants, revenue generation via entrant fees, and increase the spectator base. As promoter H. D. mentioned, "Youth and Old Timer events is cash money. They bring out other family members who pay to get in and eat and drink."

RODEO COMPETITIONS

Soul Circuit rodeos, much like mainstream rodeos, began with a grand entry. This standard ritual consisted of rodeo contestants lined up in single file on horseback circling the arena in a parade-like manner. During the grand entry both the American and Texas flags were presented to the audience. A "riderless horse," which symbolizes death in the rodeo family during the year was also a part of the procession. H. C., a former rodeo cowboy and now rodeo promoter, discussed the practice. "The riderless horse with the boots in the stirrups facing backwards symbolizes death: rider, promoter, or any individual closely tied to the rodeo. It could be one person or several individuals." Various dignitaries, as well as the rodeo promoter and stock contractor, participated in this ritual. Also, the Cowboy Prayer and salute to Old Glory was customary at most of the black rodeos.

The vast majority of Soul Circuit rodeos observed were advertised as "open competitions." This basically meant that contestants did not have to be PRCA members or affiliated with a sanctioned rodeo organization. In essence, anyone could compete if they paid the requisite event registration fee. Many of the rodeos were lengthy and loosely structured. On average competitions varied in length from 3 to 8 hours. The lengthiness of the rodeos was primarily due to two major factors: "walk-up" registration, and basic organizational structure. In an effort to increase the payout and generate additional revenue promoters often waived advanced registration. This administrative decision enabled rodeo cowboys to register for an event immediately before it began. Unfortunately, this option compromised any time schedule that was to be maintained, slowed down the rodeo, and invariably led to long breaks between events. F. W., a celebrated PRCA member and former Soul Circuit rider, commented on the aforementioned shortcomings:

I roped at all of 'em over the years: McBeth, Navasota, Madisonville, you name it. One of the problems is they're too long. I can make more money in one PRCA event than I can in a whole rodeo out here. [Also], registration should be in advance. A cowboy shouldn't be allowed to pay right before the event begins. This makes the rodeo drag.

Other cowboys expressed similar sentiments regarding the organizational structure but were less likely to be overly critical because of their limited options.

SOUL CIRCUIT/SUBTERRANEAN CIRCUIT INHIBITING FACTORS

Over the years African American cowboys were less likely to be employed in work settings where they could leave their jobs mid-week to travel to distant rodeos. Even today this is an inhibiting factor. As a result, they have primarily participated in unsanctioned weekend competitions close to home. None of the rodeos on the Soul Circuit were sanctioned by the PRCA, the largest national and international governing body of professional rodeo. Although these rodeos are viable professional competitions, the payouts are nominal and exposure is minimal; therefore, they rarely enhance the marketability of the rodeo athlete nationally. Lastly, they do not factor into the monetary standings and rankings for the PRCA.

Due to financial constraints and job stability concerns African American cowboys were more apt to participate in the smaller, closer, unsanctioned ethnic rodeos. In these competitions points and yearly financial earnings were rarely tallied, thereby making rankings impossible. The lack of meticulous record keeping, and a standardized ranking system adversely affected these cowboys because they invariably lacked the requisite documentation to qualify for the more celebrated competitions nationally.

Participation on the Soul Circuit over the years has been a viable means for honing skills but not sufficient enough to earn a living. This was often due to the limited sponsorship, which invariably impacted all aspects of the rodeo production. Sponsorship and vendor fees enable promoters to offer greater payouts, which attracts more competitors, provides better quality animals, and enhances overall marketing through diverse outlets. Thus, limited event sponsorship minimized the athletes' earning potential. Since few events were underwritten or received money from corporate sponsors, rodeo promoters relied primarily on registration fees, gate receipts, and parking to cover expenses and pay event winners. Therefore, open registration was usually practiced to accommodate late registrants to assure a larger pool of money.

This promotional strategy frequently increased the number of competitors but slowed down the rodeo. One highly successful PRCA rodeo cowboy and former Soul Circuit participant stated that he could make $7,000.00 to $8,000.00 riding in one or two PRCA competitions in the same amount of time that he could make $700.00 in a Soul Circuit competition. According to him, at this stage of his career it was not a good investment of time. Other rodeo cowboys had similar views because it is common practice for them to compete in several rodeos concurrently.

Previous segregation policies which prohibited and/or discouraged African American participation has had a lingering effect on many of the veteran competitors. On several occasions African American cowboys recalled incidents where they were not welcomed at some of the mainstream rodeos. Several recanted incidents where they were required to ride before the fans had entered the arena, while others competed after they had left. Incidents of unfair judging and the refusal to pay individuals for winning or placing were also mentioned. These and other incidents were among the reasons given for the formation of ethnic rodeos, riding clubs, and associations. Younger rodeo cowboys were less likely to experience such overt discrimination and rarely expressed such sentiments. Several veteran rodeo cowboys who participated on the Soul Circuit implied that the caliber of contestants and crowd support are far less than they used to be. They equated the present-day Soul Circuit with the latter years of the Negro Leagues when opportunities to play in Major League Baseball became a reality.

Shrewd marketing and promotional strategies have made the Soul Circuit a viable sport and entertainment option. The use of conventional modes of advertising has kept promotional cost down, as well as the staging of competitions in small rural environs. Additionally, the scheduling of nontraditional rodeo events like Jr. Roping, Old Timers Roping, and Open Break-Away have increased the pool of paying competitors and has built a potential "feeder system" into the circuit. From a sociological perspective this approach may be viewed as a form of "prole sport" (working class) "generational socialization," whereby several generations of rodeo cowboys could be competing at the same venue in the following event categories: Mutton Busting (5 and 6), Pee Wee (13 and under), Junior Roping (18 and under), Open ("Elite competition"), and Old Timers' (40 and over). Although the age requirements may vary opportunities to accommodate a range of rodeo contestants enhances the overall gate receipts. This does not include events exclusive to rodeo cowgirls like barrel racing, "ladies" breakaway roping, steer undecorating, and Pee Wee pole bending which can provide additional revenue.

Another marketing ploy and salient feature of the Soul Circuit was the rodeo dance. This commonly scheduled activity, which is covered in the rodeo admission fee, afforded both competitors and spectators an opportunity to fraternize.

It also served as an additional revenue generator for the event promoter. At many black rodeos where space permits contestants and spectators are permitted to campout and participate in a trail ride. These spectator perks add value to the admission fee and have the potential to increase attendance. Akin to the much larger Houston Livestock Show and Rodeo, which features a top entertainer each of the twenty-three nights of the rodeo, the Soul Circuit rodeo dance has attracted fans and non-fans alike. Zydeco and Rhythm and Blues were frequently the music of choice because of its ethnic lyrics and historical significance; however, as times have changed a more diverse selection has included Rap, Hip Hop, and Country and Western. Juneteenth (19th June), not 4th July, is celebrated as "Cowboy Christmas" in black rodeo circles. This historically significant date has traditionally been considered emancipation day for African Americans in Texas. And like Independence Day for mainstream rodeo, more ethnic rodeos are scheduled on Juneteenth than any other single day of the year.

Although few rodeo cowboys competing on this circuit of marginally promoted rodeos, in secluded rural hamlets, devoid of media exposure, will ever earn PRCA credentials and notoriety, they continue to perform and hone their skills. Consistent with the past, and reminiscently akin to the Negro Leagues after integration, this Subterranean Circuit has managed to maintain the vestiges of its cultural tradition and lore.

NOTE

1. Originally published as "Shadow Riders of the Subterranean Circuit: A Descriptive Account of Black Rodeo in the Texas Gulf Coast Region," by Demetrius W. Pearson, *Journal of American Culture 27*(2) (June 2004): 190–198. Reprinted with permission from John Wiley and Sons. Copyright © 1999–2021 John Wiley & Sons, Inc. All rights reserved.

REFERENCES

Blanchard, K. (1995). *The Anthropology of Sport: An Introduction.* (Rev. ed). Westport, CT: Bergin & Garvey.

Coakley, J. J. (2001). *Sport in Society: Issues and Controversies* (7th ed.). Boston, MA: McGraw-Hill.

Collins, E., & McIngvale., J. (1997, February 16). Yall and us are pardners in Texas. *Houston Chronicle*, pp. C1, C5.

Jackson, E., Jr. (2000). *Celebrating Black Cowboys in 2000* [Brochure]. Houston, TX: Clear Channel Communications.

Lawrence, E. A. (1982). *Rodeo: An Anthropologist Looks at the Wild and the Tame.* Chicago, IL: University of Chicago Press.

Newman, A. (1997, September 1). Deep in the heart of Brooklyn, cowboys and kosher food. *New York Times,* late ed., p. B1.

Pearson, D. W., & Haney C. A. (1999a). The rodeo cowboy: Cultural icon, athlete, or entrepreneur? *Journal of Sport & Social Issues 23*(3), 308–327.

Pearson, D. W., & Haney C. A. (1999b). The rodeo cowboy as an American Icon: The perceived social and cultural significance. *Journal of American Culture 22*(4), 17–21.

Professional Rodeo Cowboys Association. (1999). *Media guide* [Brochure]. Colorado Springs, CO: Professional Rodeo Cowboys Association.

PRORODEO. (2020). About the PRCA. Colorado Springs, CO: Professional Rodeo Cowboys Association. Retrieved from https://www.prorodeo.com/prorodeo/rodeo/about-the-prca

Watriss, W. (1980, December). The soul circuit. *Geo 2,* 134–150.

Chapter 7

Black in the Saddle
The Best Bull Rider You Never Saw

[1]As previously noted, the legacy of African people in the American West dates back to the sixteenth century: a period known to historians as "The Age of Exploration" or the "Elizabethan Era." This legacy is primarily due to the explorations of Estevanico, the once enslaved Moor from North Africa, who traversed the southwestern regions of the United States for Spain. In his quest to locate the Seven Cities of Cibola, Estevanico traveled through present-day Texas, New Mexico, and Arizona. He is said to have been the first black man in North America (Barr, 1996), and "the man who guided the first white explorers through the American Southwest" (Altman, 1997, p. 84). His early sixteenth-century travels stimulated and gave impetus to the explorations of Spanish explorers such as Coronado and de Soto (Asante & Mattson, 1991).

Equally of interest is the misconception that the American West was a land devoid of racial diversity. Although rarely portrayed in Western novels and motion pictures of the twentieth century, historical evidence suggests that approximately one in three cowboys were "of color" (Katz, 1996). Hence, the indigenous people of North America (i.e., Mexicans and Indigenous People), as well as descendants from Africa, helped transplanted European land barons with the livestock management business. An estimated 9,000 African Americans participated in the cattle industry and multistate drives of the late 1800s. This included some of the most notable cattle drive trails of the southwest (e.g., Chisholm, Goodnight-Loving, Western, and Shawnee). Interestingly, Michael Moore (2001), formerly executive director of the George Ranch Historical Park, confirmed the presence and prevalence of African American cowboys on the once expansive George Ranch in Richmond, TX. He stated, "virtually all of the cowboys shown in pay records of the mid-1890s were African Americans" (2001, p. 241). Yet their contributions have often been ignored, misrepresented, or omitted from sundry historical accounts. As a result, I have referred to them as "shadow riders" (Pearson, 2004, p. 102) because they were among the many trailblazers and pioneers of the West yet received little attention and notoriety. In essence, they rode in the shadows of their white cowboy counterparts.

African Americans participated in myriad roles in the American West. Among the more celebrated figures were Deputy U.S. Marshal Bass Reeves, the legendary stealth lawman and master of disguise; "Stagecoach" Mary Fields, who at the age of sixty-three was a driver of a U.S. Mail coach in Montana; James Beckwourth, the mountain man and frontier scout whose name graces the Sierra Nevada mountains (Beckwourth Pass); and the many heroic Buffalo Soldiers of the 9th and 10th Calvary as well as the 24th and 25th Infantry, who endured Spartan conditions to help open the western frontier. Perhaps the most recognizable African American figure of the old West is Bill Pickett. Born in Taylor, TX, in 1870, Pickett honed his ranching skills on the Miller Brothers' 101 Ranch in Oklahoma. Some contend that he was the greatest cowhand that ever lived. Noted for his roping and riding prowess Pickett became a box-office celebrity at rodeos and Wild West shows around the turn of the century. It is he who is credited with inventing bulldogging (steer wrestling), one of the seven major rodeo events. However, prior to his notoriety, he frequently had to dress as a Mexican toreador because of discriminatory practices toward African Americans. Pickett eventually rose to such prominence as a Wild West Show celebrity and rodeo cowboy that he became the first African American to be inducted into the National Cowboy Hall of Fame, and later the ProRodeo Hall of Fame. The overt omission and trivialization of the contributions made by people of African descent in the expansion of the western frontier has been pervasive and widespread. Yet, the voices of African American griots, scholars of Western history, and the reemergence of American rodeo as a contemporary sport form and entertainment option, have led to a reexamination of the American West.

SHADOW RIDERS: A CURSORY REVIEW OF INSTITUTIONALIZED MARGINALIZATION

For more than half of the twentieth-century African Americans were systematically denied access and opportunities to fully participate in American society. This social disenfranchisement operated at all aspects of society, including work and play. American rodeo, whose origins can be traced to festival pastimes in Mexico, evolved into a quasi-sport form in the United States during the late nineteenth century. This work-related sport form, and its prole subculture, incorporated the social and cultural norms that were pervasive in American society. As a result, even though African Americans were inextricably involved in the cattle industry, rodeo, and "the western expansion," American history and sport have frequently marginalized their contributions. The term shadow riders metaphorically refers to the many African American rodeo cowboys who participated in rodeo competitions throughout North America in the shadows of their white counterparts with little or no recognition or exposure.

With the exception of boxing, sanctioned segregation in all major American sports was the norm until the late 1940s. Yet and still sports like baseball and rodeo were participated in and influenced by minority athletes whose legacy has been largely overlooked. A classic example of this phenomenon is the Negro Leagues in baseball and the Southwestern Colored Cowboys Association in rodeo. These organizations were established by African Americans to counteract discrimination experienced in mainstream baseball and rodeo, while affording African American athletes an opportunity to hone their athletic skills, and supplement incomes. Ernest Jackson, Jr. (2000) highlighted this noteworthy point:

> Although the Professional Rodeo Cowboys Association (PRCA) never had a written policy that excluded minority competitors, it is interesting to read comments from older cowboys... reference to "the days of segregated rodeo." Until around the 1950s, the lack of black professional cowboys and some underlying racism kept most blacks from competing with whites. To combat this situation, black cowboys of the 1940s formed the Southwestern Colored Cowboys Association (SCCA). (p. 12)

Striking parallels have been addressed by researchers familiar with the nuances of these sport organizations and their impact (Pearson, 2004). For example, both served as "incubators" for early integration era African American athletes' ascendance to mainstream sport. The tutelage and guidance received in the Negro Leagues and the Southwestern Colored Cowboys Association, which orchestrated the "Soul Circuit" (or "Subterranean Circuit"), provided an invaluable resource for individuals who were denied opportunities to participate based solely on skin color. Baseball luminaries like Jackie Robinson, Larry Doby, Roy Campannella, Monte Irvin, Willie Mays, Henry Aaron, and Ernie Banks all reached the pinnacle of baseball immortality: the Baseball Hall of Fame, due in part to the grooming done in the Negro Leagues. Unfortunately the list is not nearly as replete in rodeo. To date, only Bill Pickett, Jesse Stahl, Charles Sampson, Myrtis Dightman, and Fred Whitfield have received similar honors. However, this does not devalue the salient contributions of the Soul Circuit, which consisted of a network of "loosely structured," open rodeo competitions, held primarily in small rural environs, devoid of major media coverage in Texas and Oklahoma. The competitors and spectators alike were usually minority, and primarily African Americans. These competitions drew considerable support due to the patronage of the "devotees," who were privy to watching many of the most talented minority rodeo cowboys in the world.

Unfortunately, this collection of talent was a by-product of sanctioned segregation because minority cowboys (akin to their Negro League counterparts) were frequently denied entry into mainstream rodeos due to unwritten policies. These exclusionary societal norms inhibited the skill development, exposure, and revenue generating capacity of many aspiring African American rodeo cowboys. Even when mainstream sport forms began to drop their exclusionary bans, and the federal government prohibited segregation in the military, much like the Emancipation Proclamation, the message was not readily disseminated and implemented throughout the south. As a result, discriminatory practices and segregated competitions continued. Even when African Americans were permitted to participate in integrated rodeos they were forced to ride before the spectators arrived at the arena or after the main competition had concluded. At major fat stock shows and rodeos like Fort Worth and Houston African American cowboys could only compete, and like spectators attend, on one specific day.

WILLIE THOMAS: AN UNHERALDED CELEBRITY AND PIONEER OF SORTS

An unfortunate product of this discriminatory treatment and "racial impositioning" within American rodeo was Willie Thomas. A Fort Bend County native, and one of four siblings who was born to domestic workers on the legendary George Ranch (Richmond, TX) in 1930, Thomas knew a few things about the not so subtle indignities of "rodeoing while black." However, prior to his rodeo involvement, disenfranchisement for him and countless African Americans in the south was the norm. Educated in the segregated schools of nearby Booth, TX, and relegated to vision in one eye due to a childhood accident, Thomas never experienced a "level playing field." He was often the lone African American contestant at integrated rodeos in the late-1940s and 1950s. In an interview conducted on his ranch in 2007, Thomas stated that he was the first African American to compete in the Houston Livestock Show and Rodeo: the largest and most lucrative rodeo in the world, the Fort Worth Fat Stock Show and Rodeo, as well as others. Interestingly he was frequently lauded as much for his genteel disposition as his deft bull riding. Unfortunately "jaundiced-eye" judging adversely impacted his scores. As a result, on many occasions he left the arena with far less money than his skills warranted. Thomas shown bull riding at the Tulsa Stampede (Figure 7.1), once wryly commented that in order

Figure 7.1 Willie Thomas on #01 (Beutler Bros.), Tulsa Stampede, 1962. Ferrell Butler, 1962, silver gelatin print. *Source:* PRCA Rodeo Sports News Photographic Collection, Dickinson Research Center, National Cowboy & Western Heritage Museum. 1998.008.8062.

to get a chance to place in the money, due to the biased judging, he had to ride a bull until it stopped bucking.

> I would have to ride 'em till he lay down. They did you so bad. They treat you so bad during those days you don't want to talk about 'em. Sometimes I would be at a rodeo from 8:00 p.m. till 4:00 a.m. [because they] made you ride after the main rodeo competition was over. The judging would be so unfair. (personal communication, March 2, 2007)

A former bareback rider and rodeo promoter stated that one of the ways in which biased judging manifested itself was during the "mark out" in the saddle bronc and bareback riding events. Although Thomas acknowledged this shortcoming, he always reminded cowboys he mentored that: "You can't ride and judge at the same time" (KI-HC, personal communication, March 29, 2006). Yet and still, these early setbacks did not deter Thomas from pursuing his passion for rodeoing.

Thomas' rodeo career received a major boost when he was befriended by "The Singing Cowboy," Gene Autry, who was a frequent guest at the George Ranch in the mid-1950s. Throughout the 1950s Thomas worked and rodeoed with Autry's traveling rodeo company. It was also during these years that Thomas began to carve out a name for himself in and around rodeo circles. While many African American cowboys were riding on the Soul Circuit Thomas had already earned his PRCA credentials and was competing at the highest level of rodeo competition. His burgeoning rodeo career and odyssey took him throughout the United States and various parts of Canada (e.g., Calgary Stampede). This was often a lonely and dangerous odyssey because many of the major sport forms had only recently begun to desegregate. Some teams, like the Boston Red Sox, had yet to employ an African American player. And with the exception of Fritz Pollard (during the 1920s) none of the mainstream sport leagues were coached or managed by an African American. It is also important to note that many hotels, restaurants, transportation systems, and public amenities throughout the country had yet to be desegregated. Even those that were integrated were not always accommodating. Thomas lamented about his treatment even though he does not appear to harbor much resentment or bitterness:

> I couldn't get a room. You'd get there and have to sleep in the truck. It was rough. They'd serve them [white cowboys] and wouldn't serve me. I'd be shame to go eat with somebody because I knew they wouldn't feed me. You'd have to find a black place, [but] they wouldn't be open. (personal communication, March 2, 2007)

Many who initially started down the rodeo trail with Thomas opted to stay closer to home, in more hospitable environs, where life was more predictable. Thomas, at times, even grew tired of the offensive remarks, biased judging, and discriminatory treatment but managed to persevere. He contended that bull riding was a gift to him and that there wasn't a bull that he couldn't ride. This level of self-confidence and assurance often served as the impetus for him to compete, in spite of the adversities. A veteran rodeo cowboy and Texas Rodeo Cowboy Hall of Fame inductee agreed, "If a bull stands still and Willie gets right the bull can't throw him" (KI-CW, personal communication, September 6, 2004).

His knack for riding some of the most dangerous and recalcitrant bulls on the rodeo circuit was somewhat legendary. A long-time associate, former rodeo cowboy and promoter, recalled Thomas' bull riding prowess being put to a test early in his rodeo career. He stated that a prominent World Champion rodeo cowboy unimpressed by Thomas' previous bull rides and unorthodox style of putting his rope on bulls exclaimed, "watch this 'nigger-wreck'"

(KI-HC, personal communication, March 29, 2006). Although Thomas did not win any money in the event, contrary to speculation he didn't wreck (bucked off) either. Interestingly, several individuals took note of his skills and at the conclusion of the rodeo challenged him to ride four re-ride bulls for $10.00 each. Thomas accepted the challenge, rode all four bulls, and left the arena with an extra $40.00 in his pocket. At other times, stock promoters and contractors were ambivalent toward Thomas drawing their advertised "un-rideable" bulls in fear that he would ride them, thus lowering their value and marketability. During an interview session related to his uncanny ability to ride the distance, Thomas remembered a dangerous bull that was destined to be retired because it had a penchant for breaking bull riders' noses. When asked to elaborate he nonchalantly said, "I rode 'em" (personal communication, March 2, 2007). A nationally respected PRCA Hall of Fame cowboy and announcer, who witnessed many of Thomas' rides, stated that he went a period of three years without being bucked off a bull. Thomas disputed the claim and stated it was actually five years. The discrepancy may be due in part to Thomas' ability to participate in PRCA-sanctioned rodeos as well as unsanctioned, open, Soul Circuit competitions. This provision was afforded minority riders by the PRCA because the Soul Circuit served as a "training ground."

DOWN THE RODEO TRAIL

Much has changed in America and the world of sport over the last 50 years. However, in the not so distant past, "People of Color" and African Americans in particular encountered a myriad of problems when traveling through various parts of the United States. In some cities and towns, especially in the South, public facilities were segregated (i.e., restrooms, water fountains, restaurants, and parks), accommodations (i.e., hotels and motels) were off limits, and rodeo participation was discriminatory at best. Such was the case for Willie Thomas when he took to the rode to rodeo. He and others who traveled with him recall some of their experiences.

> I remember we was on the road and stopped in Beard, TX, to get a room. They wouldn't let us stay in the hotel, so we had to drive many miles before we could find a place that would let us get a room. (KI-CW, personal communication, September 6, 2004)

The discriminatory treatment invariably impacted the performance of African American cowboys who attempted to travel the PRCA circuit. An interviewee recalled a situation that Willie Thomas encountered while on the rodeo circuit:

> Willie entered a rodeo competition somewhere in Texas [Kansas] and made hotel reservations in the town where the rodeo was to be held. When he got to the hotel, they refused him a room. After sitting and laying on a bench much of the night he was told by police to move along. He walked to the rodeo arena and slept on the bleachers all night. He competed the next day. (KI-HC, personal communication, March 29, 2006)

On another occasion a similar situation occurred, but accommodations were afforded the African American rodeo cowboys, albeit not what they had anticipated.

> We were going to Harrisburg, PA, and stopped in London, OH. Hotel reservations had been made in advance. When we went to check into the hotel the woman [desk attendant] said there were no vacancies. The sign outside said vacancies. After several attempts to get a room we decided to leave. She called the Sheriff. Before we left a sheriff approached and inquired about the problem. We told him and he said there wasn't much he could do. He said, y'all can come down to the jailhouse. Because we were tired and didn't know where else to go, we took him up on the offer. It was the best offer we got. *WE SLEPT IN A JAIL CELL* [italics added]! (KI-FG, personal communication, September 6, 2006)

Thomas remembered the incident and added that it was eight degrees below zero, and the only option was to sleep in the truck. Unfortunately, this was the plight of many African American rodeo cowboys when they traveled the rodeo circuit.

RODEO VENUES AND ARBITRARY GATEKEEPERS

For the faithful few African American rodeo cowboys who did compete at PRCA-sanctioned rodeos during the 1950s and 1960s traveling was only part of their woes. Many found difficulty in accessing rodeo venues once they had registered for events. For example:

> In Center, TX, they didn't let blacks in the fairground. So we were not initially allowed to come in. A white man at the gate said, Negroes' night was on Tuesday. Willie told him to call the headman in Denver, CO. The headman insisted that they let Willie ride. He rode after the crowd left and won the bull riding event. (KI-SF, personal communication, September 2, 2004)

The aforementioned practice, whereby African American rodeo cowboys competed before the spectators arrived or after they left the arena, was quite common. Unfortunately, on various occasions the paying spectators missed some of the most spectacular rides. Even if the opportunity was afforded, and the rodeo cowboy rode well enough to earn some money, he was not always assured of receiving it. Willie Thomas recalled having "placed in the money" in the bareback event at an integrated rodeo. However, when he went to the pay window, they refused to give him his money. He asked a white friend if he would get his money. He did and a lasting relationship developed over the years. Tragically, the latter's World Champion bull riding son was killed during a rodeo competition in 1989. Interestingly, a movie was released in 1994 that chronicled the bull rider's life.

Austin, TX, was a "bad town to rodeo in," according to Thomas (personal communication, May 18, 2007). The state's capital city was one of the many southern cities steeped in the throes of tradition and discrimination.

> Worst town in the world to go to a rodeo in. I won the bull riding competition [either 1955 or 1959] but couldn't go in the room to collect my money. A lawman had to get the money because they wouldn't let me in the room. (personal communication, March 2, 2007, and May 18, 2007)

At other rodeo arenas he encountered the same kind of treatment that Jackie Robinson was subjected to in major league ballparks.

> Back at some of the white shows [rodeos] they would throw paper and spit at him. Willie never gave up. He kept on ridin [sic]. He didn't get a fair judge at many white shows, but he couldn't do nothin [sic] about it. He be the only black ridin [sic]. (KI-PB, personal communication, September 6, 2007)

In spite of the adversities and racial indignities incurred, Thomas maintained a reserved demeanor. As a result, he was accorded a certain level of respect from his rodeo counterparts. A veteran professional rodeo announcer and Texas Rodeo Cowboy Hall of Fame inductee referred to Thomas in the following manner: "Class guy. He handled segregation. It was tough for those boys during that time. He had to ride after the rodeo in the 1940s in order to win money" (KI-DW, personal communication, May 17, 2006).

COMPETITION: JUST GIVE ME A CHANCE

Rodeo is a sport whereby cowboys compete with and against the animals they ride, as well as other cowboys. Thomas found out very early that the event judges were a major factor in the scoring equation. Many of the key informants who were interviewed spoke openly or alluded to the bias judging toward African American rodeo cowboys. They frequently mentioned that lesser skilled rodeo cowboys often received higher scores than Thomas and other African American contestants.

> There were times when we would ride for 10–11 seconds get throwed [sic] off and then the whistle would blow. The judging was so unfair. When I rode White Lightning, I should have won the pot. They put a white guy in who didn't ride well but got a higher score. (KI-CW, personal communication, September 6, 2004)

In a written statement, a former rodeo cowboy and judge corroborated the plight of African American cowboys with respect to biased judging. He wrote:

> During the 1950s and '60s when I rodeoed, I had a chance to watch Willie in the bull riding. I also judged some of the rodeos which Willie was entered in. In my opinion he was one of the best during that time. Being a black cowboy rodeoing during those years was tough. If Willie was going now, it would not surprise me at all if he won the world. (KI-JH, personal communication, January 9, 1999)

Mid-twentieth-century rodeo was susceptible to such practices due to the subjective and arbitrary nature of the sport's scoring system. In addition, scores were not immediately posted after each ride. During Thomas' career scores were usually posted after the competition was over; thus, scores could be manipulated in favor of certain competitors. A former rodeo cowboy and promoter recanted a story in which Willie Thomas rode a bull for approximately 15 seconds. After tiring he stepped off. Shortly after, the buzzer sounded. A local lawman approached the judges and remarked, "You know that was a damn shame the way y'all did that fella" (KI-HC, personal communication, March 29, 2006).

> Thomas recalled an incident in Lake Charles, LA, in the late 1950s where he won the first go round in the bull riding competition, but when he went to prepare for the second go round he was forced to leave the arena. "They wouldn't give me my second bull. Rodeo officials told me to leave the arena. They sent the high sheriff over to get me. I couldn't get my money. He escorted me to the Texas line, and told me don't come back or the Ku Klux Klan would kill me." (personal communication, March 18, 2007)

Closer to home in a rodeo at Rosenberg, TX, the promoters were so fearful that Thomas would win the bull riding competition that they asked him not to ride and refunded his registration fee. This was a most unfortunate situation for Thomas, a local contestant (and maybe more so for those who were deprived of the privilege of watching him ride), but it also served as an acknowledgment of his bull riding prowess.

ARGUABLY THE BEST

Regardless of the sport, when an athlete is selected as the "best" or "greatest" a firestorm of debate ensues shortly thereafter. Surely such would be the case if one were to definitively proclaim that Willie Thomas was the best bull rider ever. Most would dismiss the statement as ludicrous because he never appeared in the National Finals Rodeo (NFR) or had not won any World Championships in bull riding. Yet, Satchel Paige never won a Cy Young Award or led the major leagues in victories but is considered to be one of the greatest pitchers in baseball history. Enshrined in the Baseball Hall of Fame in 1971, Paige's plaque resides alongside other baseball luminaries who didn't play with or against him. Some were best served by not having played against him during the height of his career as their statistics would not be as good. In spite of his limited stint in mainstream baseball, Paige was still revered by baseball aficionados as one of the game's greatest pitchers.

However, based upon statements made during the interviews, letters supporting Thomas' candidacy for the National Cowboy Hall of Fame, informal conversations at various rodeos, and archived documents, a case can be made. One interviewee stated, "There was no one you could compare him to. [He was an] excellent rodeo cowboy. He was a finesse rider, who rode better than Myrtis" (KI-TL, personal communication, February 7, 2007). The bull rider referred to in this instance is multi-NFR qualifier Myrtis Dightman, who was the first African American to participate in the National Finals and place in the bull riding event. Dightman concurred with the aforementioned statement, and acknowledged Thomas' bull riding prowess in a written statement:

> He was a great cowboy and an excellent bull rider. I always thought that he was much better than I could ever be. Sometime I sit and I think that Willie did not get the recognition he deserved because he was too early. If he could start over again, no doubt, he would be the world's greatest, but we know that it's impossible to do. (personal communication, January 12, 1999)

Another veteran rodeo cowboy, who met Thomas at a Madison Square Garden rodeo in 1955 and participated in several NFR competitions, attested to the exceptional bull riding skills of Thomas as well. An excerpt from a letter he wrote, supporting Thomas' induction into the National Cowboy Hall of Fame read as follows:

In the fourteen years I was around him, I don't think he bucked off a half dozen bulls. He was not a good bull rider; he was a Great Bull Rider. I put him in the class with Mr. Harry Thompkins. Had he been a white man, I think he would have been a World's Champion. I made the National Finals Rodeo the first six years as a bull rider and I didn't ride near as good as Willie. About the only way a black man could win anything back in the '50s and '60s was to be the only one to make the whistle. Therefore he didn't travel much. I consider Willie to be the bull rider that Bill Pickett was to bull dogging. (KI-JG, personal communication, January 1, 1999)

Thompkins, a five-time World Champion bull rider, noted that Thomas rode as well as 90 percent of the cowboys bull riding during his career. He also maintained that African American cowboys, in spite of their rodeo prowess, were often treated unfairly (personal communication, January 3, 1999).

One can only imagine the success and notoriety that Thomas might have experienced had he been afforded an opportunity to fully participate in mainstream rodeo. Some of the individuals who witnessed his rides noted his fluidity and style, while others remarked about his poise and control. "He was the best sporting cowboy in the business. He'd ride so easy that the judges thought the bull wasn't very good" (KI-SF, personal communication, September 2, 2004). Another veteran rodeo cowboy and prominent promoter, who saw Thomas ride in Kendleton, TX, in the 1950s stated:

He was the classiest black bull rider in the world. Myrtis was powerful; Willie had finesse. Probably the best bull rider [of his time] black or white. Everybody in the rodeo business wanted to see him ride. Willie Thomas could have won the World Championship many times. (KI-CH, personal communication, September 7, 2004)

Those that rode with and against him, as well as those that watched, were well aware of his exceptional talent. "Willie and I rode in a lot of rodeos together. He was just as good as those in the Hall of Fame and better. Boy could win some money anywhere he go" (KI-RJ, personal communication, July 15, 2006). The most salient assessment and acclimation of Thomas' rodeo prowess were highlighted during a telephone interview:

Tremendous bull rider. Top 5 all-time. He could ride nearly every bull. I frequently kid [rodeo] cowboys by saying, if Willie had been white, we would never have heard of Jim Shoulders. [Willie] might have been the best bull rider who ever lived. (KI-DW, personal communication, May 17, 2006)

According to the interviewee, ranking Thomas among the top 5 bull riders of all-time would place him with rodeo legends such as George Paul, Freckles Brown (1962 Bull Riding World Champion and first to ride "Tornado the Unrideable Bull"), Harry Thompkins (8-time World Champion), and Jim Shoulders (16-time World Champion). Needless to say, Thomas is arguably the most unheralded bull riding great that has ever entered the rodeo arena.

CONCLUSION

As stated at the outset, very little has been written about African American rodeo cowboys and their pre- and post-integration rodeo experiences. This study is unique in several respects because it highlights and discusses the travails and triumphs of arguably the best bull rider in the history of the sport; provides a cursory overview of African American involvement in the settling of the western frontier; and documents some of the verbatim statements of individuals who witnessed and/or were impacted by discriminatory practices in rodeo and American society at large. It is important to note that the majority of the key informants interviewed for this study rode, judged, watched, or announced rodeos in which Willie Thomas participated in during his career. Equally noteworthy were the interviewees that included PRCA Hall of Fame inductees, prominent stock contractors, rodeo promoters, civic leaders, and long-time devotees. Many of the interviewees were 60 years old or more and witnessed what they articulated. Documents reviewed for the study were obtained from private collections and public archives (i.e., libraries, museums, halls of fame, etc.). To confirm, disconfirm, and clarify information secured from the interviews systematic cross referencing of statements and member checks were employed.

The significance of this study may be threefold: (1) it offers up a narrative account of the rodeo experiences of an uncelebrated and under recognized rodeo pioneer, (2) corroborates some of the existing historical research pertaining to African Americans and the West, and (3) contributes to the sport legacy of African American rodeo cowboys. Interestingly, it was most fitting that on February 14, 2004, Willie Thomas was inducted into the Texas Rodeo Cowboy Hall of Fame, an honor well deserved and long overdue. And on May 19, 2005, the Texas House of Representatives passed a resolution (H.R. No. 1455) on the floor of the state capitol honoring the legendary rodeo cowboy. This was an ironic circumstance because it was in Austin, TX, back in the 1950s, where Thomas was denied access to the room in which he was to pick up his prize money for winning the bull riding event at a PRCA-sanctioned rodeo competition. Metaphorically, for those who engaged in biased judging, benefited from the discriminatory treatment, and verbally abused and taunted Thomas over the years, he may be seen as an itch that can't be scratched. His mere presence may elicit and remind individuals of the biased judging, racial indignities, and unethical activities they perpetrated on him during his rodeo career. Over 50 years have passed since his initial professional bull riding victory, yet and still Thomas is winning. Currently he serves as a living legacy and a reminder of what life was like for an African American rodeo cowboy, who opted to compete throughout the country at the highest level of competition, regardless of the personal sacrifices and adversities. One veteran rodeo cowboy attempted to express Thomas' legacy, greatness, and contributions to the sport of rodeo in a draft letter seeking a presidential acknowledgment. In the letter he metaphorically referred to Thomas as a bearing fruit tree, and from that tree came Myrtis Dightman, Sr. From the Myrtis Dightman, Sr. tree came Charles Sampson. All were products of Willie Thomas, the root of the tree, shown in one of his championship belt buckles (Figure 7.2).

Figure 7.2 Bull Rider and Living Legend Willie Thomas, Richmond, TX, 2016. *Source:* Courtesy of Andrea Robbins & Max Becher © 2016.

NOTE

1. Copyright 2009. From "Black in the Saddle: The Best Bull Rider You Never Saw," by Demetrius W. Pearson in *Racial Structure & Radical Politics in the African Diaspora, Africana Studies*, Volume 3, pp. 183–196. Reproduced by permission of Taylor and Francis Group, LLC, a division of Informa plc; permission conveyed through Copyright Clearance Center, Inc.

REFERENCES

Altman, S. (1997). *The Encyclopedia of African-American Heritage*. New York, NY: Facts-On-File.
Asante, M. K., & Mattson, M. T. (1991). *Historical and Cultural Atlas of African Americans*. New York, NY: Macmillan.
Barr, A. (1996). *A History of African Americans in Texas, 1528–1995* (2nd ed.). Norman, OK: University of Oklahoma Press.
Jackson, E., Jr. (2000). *Celebrating Black Cowboys in 2000* [Brochure]. Houston, TX: Houston Clear Channel Communications.
Katz, W. L. (1996). *The Black West*. New York, NY: Simon.
Massey, S. R. (Ed.). (2000). *Black Cowboys of Texas*. College, TX: Texas A&M Press.
Moore, M. R. (2001). *Settlers, Slaves, Sharecroppers and Stockhands: A Texas Plantation-Ranch, 1824–1896*. Unpublished master's thesis, University of Houston, Houston, TX.
Pearson, D. W. (2004). Shadow riders of the subterranean circuit: A descriptive account of Black rodeo in the Texas Gulf Coast region. *The Journal of American Culture, 27*(2), 190–198.
Porter, K. W. (1970). *The Negro on the American Frontier*. New York, NY: Arno.

Chapter 8

The New Millennium
Black Rodeo and New Jack Cowboys

In spite of the democratic façade within contemporary sport, there are still considerable challenges inhibiting black cowboys' access to professional rodeo. Abe Morris offers a cursory historical account of *The Modern Black Cowboy* and an assessment of some of the obstacles faced in Don Russell's (2016) self-published *Cowboys of Color* pictorial. He contends that because rodeo is not a mainstream sport like basketball and football in African American households, it stands to reason that many black youths do not see themselves as rodeo cowboys. Much like the past such factors as training opportunities, quality competition animals, and financial resources to subsidize their entrepreneurial endeavors (i.e., feed bills, fuel costs, vet expenses, entry fees, food, and lodging) are still lacking. Thus, the lack of corporate sponsorship, which adversely impacts the majority of rodeo cowboys is an enormous obstacle for black cowboys. This roadblock has been a perpetual problem for black athletes regardless of their respective sport. As Robert Woods in *Social Issues in Sport* (2016) states, corporate sponsorship has often eluded black athletes, even the most successful ones throughout history. He cites the difficulty former tennis star and Olympian Zina Garrison had in landing a clothing endorsement contract for much of her career while ranked fourth in the world. Woods elaborates on the corporate sponsorship perspective which has changed little in sports that garner limited attention in black households:

> Twenty years ago, companies saw little value in positioning Garrison as a role model for advertising their clothes because few African Americans were interested in tennis. Sponsors support the sports that attract participants or spectators who most closely parallel the target consumers of their product. (2016, p. 57)

Because the rodeo cowboy is a solo entrepreneur and incurs all of the expenses within his sport, corporate sponsorship is vitally necessary in order to enhance the likelihood of success and career longevity.

Other sociocultural factors that must be considered include the continual migration of black families from rural environs with farm animals to urban areas; and the perceived upward mobility via sport in highly televised mainstream sport forms (e.g., football and basketball) that traditionally provide early instruction and equipment for participants. These sport offerings are often nominal in cost or free of charge. The rewards for the fortunate few who opt to play these sports can be most rewarding; however, the odds are heavily stacked against them.

From a psychological perspective, the paucity of role models and images of black cowboys can play a significant role as well. Unfortunately, since so very few black rodeo cowboys are competing at the PRCA level, which receives the most print, broadcast media coverage, sponsorship, and endorsement opportunities, black youths find it most difficult to gravitate toward rodeo and pursue it as a career pathway contrary to football and basketball where prospective role models are abundant. Each of these sports whether at the collegiate or professional level have a significant percentage of black athletes. Also, they tend to be more accessible whether the aspiring athlete lives in an urban or rural setting. It is equally important to note that even though access may be greater due to the dismantling of Jim Crow laws and overt discrimination, more sport opportunities play a significant role in the choices young black athletes make as well. Lastly, since rodeo perceptually does not appear to be as "chic" and contemporary as basketball and football, and the Hollywood Western no longer captivates the American public as it had prior to the 1960s, it stands to reason that rodeo will not be the sport of choice in most black communities.

FLAG BEARERS AND NEW JACK BLACK COWBOYS

Regardless of the lack of representation at the highest levels of professional rodeo, the black rodeo cowboy is still alive and well in the twenty-first century. It is important to note that the vast majority of black cowboys continue to hail from Oklahoma and Texas, with the latter boasting the largest rodeo contingent in the world. Home grown Texans like youthful bull riding upstart Ezekiel Mitchell (Rockport, TX) and calf ropers Corey Solomon (Prairie View, TX), veteran Bud Ford (Mansfield, TX), and legendary Fred Whitfield (Hockley, TX) are the proverbial flag bearers. They form the elite Texas contingent of black rodeo cowboys currently competing at the highest level of the sport since the recent retirement of two-time Professional Bull Riders

(PBR) finals qualifier Neil Holmes. Each has been mentored and/or inspired by black rodeo cowboys who competed much of the time on the Soul Circuit/Subterranean Circuit. Their perseverance and relentless pursuit of the rodeo life has inspired a generation of new millennial black rodeo cowboys who may not experience the social indignities as their predecessors, but are keenly aware of the stares and racist statements made by individuals seeing black men wearing cowboy hats competing in rodeos.

In 2018, after 10 years in the sport, Neil Holmes hung up his spurs. He was one of a few black rodeo cowboys riding bulls in the PBR, but is at peace with himself and his current rodeo involvement. Holmes followed his passion even though he never considered himself a cowboy because he was never involved in farming or ranching. Therefore, he saw himself strictly as a bull rider. A top 35 rider in the PBR during much of his career, Holmes walked away from the arena as a competitor to work with the PBR's community outreach program. He has spearheaded a campaign to teach youngsters, particularly disadvantaged, inner-city minority youths about Western heritage. Holmes has welcomed the challenge and views it as an opportunity to expose kids unfamiliar with Western culture and rodeo by taking them behind the scenes to meet the riders and production staff. He has also served as a PBR representative to host the *Believe in Tomorrow Children's Foundation,* which is a community service project designed to build relationships with critically ill children and their families through rodeo. Holmes believes it to be an honor to share his story as a black cowboy as well as those who preceded him in the arena.

Ezekiel Mitchell has stepped into the void left by Holmes, and is the latest black bull riding sensation at the elite PBR level. He is currently the only black bull rider competing on the PBR rodeo circuit. "Blue" as he is known by friends, is an admitted self-taught bull rider through "how to" You Tube videos by former PBR star Dustin Elliot. In lieu of live bulls to practice on, Mitchell and a friend "jimmy rigged" a makeshift bucking barrel from a welded car suspension as his primary training device. Although short on the requisite training equipment and encouragement from family members who wished he would pursue an alternative career pathway, Mitchell's determination and athletic prowess as a former track and football athlete has had something to do with his meteoric bull riding success. During his brief stint in the PBR, he has been ranked as high as number two in the world, has won eight bull riding competitions, and amassed $228,000 in earnings. This is an incredible accomplishment for a rodeo cowboy without any formal training and less than three years on the PBR circuit. Rodeo aficionados believe Mitchell has the potential to be a top performer for years to come barring injuries, and a celebrity outside the arena as well.

His mild disposition and ability to block out some of the distractions black cowboys have had to endure and encounter on the circuit has boded well for the young bull rider. Although bull riding and rodeoing while black does not evoke and elicit the venomous racist epithets and behaviors once incurred by Soul Circuit/Subterranean Circuit cowboys of the past, Mitchell is keenly aware of the whispers, stares, and uncomplimentary statements oftentimes made by old-timers who are mired in the past. Blue Mitchell contends growing up always wanting to be a cowboy has somehow taught him to ignore the hateful comments and move forward while acknowledging his responsibility to the youth. He has found solace knowing there were elite bull riders who looked like him, albeit few, riding on the mainstream rodeo circuits in the past. The likes of home grown multi-PRCA National Finals qualifier and Hall of Famer Myrtis Dightman, Neil Holmes two-time PBR finalist, and California transplant Charles Sampson, who became the PRCA World Champion bull riding in 1982, inspire him to uphold the black cowboy legacy and see it continue.

Corey Solomon, the son of former tie-down roper Larry Solomon, Sr., is among a small contingent of black cowboys who grew up on a ranch, in a calf roping family. The Solomon family is so entrenched in the sport that they annually promote a Thanksgiving calf roping rodeo which is one of the more prominent ethnic rodeos in southeast Texas. They also serve as a stock contractor by providing calves for smaller rodeos through their LS Cattle Company in Prairie View, TX. Solomon's dream as a youngster watching PRCA calf roping champions like Cody Ohl, Joe Beaver, and Fred Whitfield was to someday make the Houston Livestock Show and Rodeo, which he eventually did. As a high school sophomore Solomon set a Texas state record with a 7.1 second tie-down run. He became a PRCA member in 2009 and has certainly made a name for himself on the professional rodeo circuit. Solomon has competed throughout North America over the past decade and has won several of the most prestigious rodeo competitions in the world including the Wainwright (Alberta) Stampede, Silver Spurs Rodeo, and was co-champion at the legendary Prescott Frontier Days. He is also a multiple Wrangler NFR qualifier, and with the exception of Fred Whitfield is arguably the best black calf roper in the world. To date, his PRCA career earnings according to RODEOTAX.COM *"The Buck Stops Here"* exceeds one million dollars (PRCA, 2019).

Veteran tie-down calf roper Bud Ford, who has been roping steers for more than two decades, is another southeast Texas rodeo cowboy that has also had his share of success. A PRCA cardholder since 1995, Ford has competed throughout the country. He stated in a *Mansfield Now Magazine* (2017) interview article titled "No Tying Him Down" that he competed in 100 rodeos alone in 1996 including the National Finals Rodeo in Las Vegas. His trip to the NFR was preceded by his calf roping championship at the prestigious Fort Worth Stock Show. In 1998, he qualified and won the calf roping event at the

Houston Livestock Show and Rodeo. This was a major accomplishment for a black rodeo cowboy who honed his skills on the Soul Circuit/Subterranean Circuit to win at the largest rodeo competition in the world. Satisfied with his national success Ford left the PRCA circuit and opted to compete locally in order to stay close to home and raise his two daughters. They have since graduated from college and are employed as social workers. Ford acknowledges that he had help along the way. His dad taught him how to rope during his formative years at the Kowbell Rodeo Arena, which he ran for 35 years. Ford says late owner Jack Ratjen is deserving of credit for making Kowbell available to him, as well as other aspiring rodeo cowboys and world champions over the years. He contends that it kept a lot of people out of trouble. Ford also acknowledges the help and support given him from longtime friend and Weatherford College rodeo coach Johnny Emmons, who he competed with and against during the early years, as well as the many people who allowed him to use their horses in competition. Cleo Hearn, founder of the Cowboys of Color rodeo series, is another individual Ford is grateful to for assisting him throughout his career. In deference to Hearn, Ford frequently competes in Cowboys of Color rodeos. Much like those who mentored him Ford spends time teaching young cowboys roping skills in a small arena on family property. "I love to help those kids," he said. "Roping is not on PlayStation 4, though. It's real. And now, you've got kids 12, 13 years old roping in 7 seconds" (Mauch, 2017, p. 11).

Without a doubt one of the greatest rodeo cowboys in the history of the sport and the most celebrated contemporary African American in the PRCA is Fred Whitfield. Affectionately known as "Moon," a name bestowed upon him by his grandfather, Whitfield started roping at the age of seven while following the son (Roy) of his mother's employer—Don Moffitt. In his autobiography *Gold Buckles Don't Lie: The Untold Tale of Fred Whitfield* (2014), Whitfield candidly speaks about his dysfunctional family that included a dad who drank constantly, was often abusive to his mother, and was eventually sent to prison for murder when he was 10 or 11 years of age. In an interview with Paul Wachter in 2016, Whitfield stated, "When he finally went away to prison, it was like thank God he's out of here" (para. 30). Ironically, not knowing otherwise, he perceived his family structure to be the norm.

Fred Whitfield seemed to take naturally to calf roping as a youth. His calf roping prowess was honed at youth rodeos, as well as local amateur and national Bill Pickett circuit rodeos. The Bill Pickett rodeo circuit was established in 1984 with the express purpose of developing African American rodeo cowboys. Although strapped for cash and without the requisite resources to seriously compete like a quality horse, a road worthy vehicle, a trailer, and entry fee money, Whitfield obtained support from childhood friend Roy Moffitt and his family. They lent him their horses, truck, trailer, and paid his entry fees. A grateful Whitfield acknowledged their unwavering support in an interview for *The Undefeated*: "Roy and his family were great to me.... When I couldn't rub two rusty nickels together, he gave me an open checkbook" (Wachter, 2016, para. 32). Whitfield became an instant success in the PRCA and qualified for the NFR in his first year on the circuit. He became only the second rookie to qualify for the PRCA's most prestigious rodeo. A year later he won the calf roping world championship, the first of his eight gold buckles.

Having acquired his PRCA membership card in 1990, Whitfield is now a seasoned veteran in the sport, and is unquestionably the most successful black cowboy who ever entered the rodeo arena. To date, Whitfield has qualified for the Wrangler NFR, which is often referred to as the Super Bowl of rodeo, twenty times and has won eight world titles. With the exception of bull rider Charlie Sampson, Whitfield is the lone African American to win a world title. His rodeo event versatility was highlighted in 1999 when he won the World All-Around title: an honor bestowed upon a cowboy who is most successful in two or more events. He is considered both a legend and an outlier within the sport of rodeo. Whitfield has won millions of dollars in the arena but is one of a handful of black cowboys competing at the highest level of the sport. His rodeo success has brought, fame, fortune, endorsement opportunities, and a recent autobiography. He has competed in most every elite PRCA-sanctioned rodeo in the United States and Canada over the past two decades with resounding success. According to his PRCA biography, he became the third PRCA cowboy in the history of the sport to reach the $3 million-dollar career threshold in 2011 (PRCA, 2019).

In spite of his rodeo success, in what is perceived to be a more open and diverse American sport culture, Whitfield has experienced some of the same racial adversities as his black predecessors. Although the inability to take lodging in towns hosting rodeos, eat in nearby restaurants, and use service station restrooms are things of the past, Whitfield has still been the target of racial taunts, epithets, and pranks because of his skin color. At one particular rodeo in Las Vegas some prankster entered the horse stalls prior to the rodeo and cut off the tail of his mare. Therefore, on occasion, he has had to fight habitually harassing cowboys and for a time, in the mid-1990s, hired bodyguards to protect himself. Whitfield has responded to the N-word yelled from the stands in less accepting environs and competing cowboys by winning. Unfortunately, his success in the arena and personal lifestyle have led to petty jealousies between him and other cowboys. As a result, some choose not to talk to him, which tends to fuel his drive to win even more.

Along with his many championship belt buckles, saddles, and miscellaneous prizes, Fred Whitfield has been inducted into the ProRodeo Hall of

Fame, Texas Cowboy Hall of Fame, National Multicultural Western Heritage Museum, and Hall of Fame, to name a few. Whitfield's success in the arena has afforded him an honor few rodeo cowboys achieve. In 1996 he signed an endorsement contract, allegedly on a napkin, with little known CINCH Jeans—a company that had initially sold jeans from the back of a pickup. Whitfield became the first professional rodeo cowboy to join the now coveted international cowboy outfitter and helped market the "Green Label" fit jean. His celebrity status and that of fellow calf roper Cody Ohl have propelled the company to unprecedented heights. Currently, many of the top rodeo cowboys wear one of the many signature model CINCH jeans.

A NEW NORMAL

Although they do not share the limelight with the more notable PRCA black rodeo cowboys, there is still a strong contingent of African American cowboys competing in local Soul Circuit/Subterranean Circuit rodeos, which are often in and around a 250-mile radius of the cowboy's hometown. A cursory analysis of the black rodeo cowboy competing on the Soul Circuit/Subterranean Circuit reveals much about the cultural significance of rodeo among a marginalized group of people. As one might expect change has occurred within black rodeo with respect to the competitors and organizational innerworkings. However, many of the same vintage arenas host black rodeos while venues once off limits to black rodeo promoters and cowboys have since opened their doors to cash in on the potential revenues that can be accrued. This is evident through the leasing of rodeo arenas like George Ranch (Richmond, TX), Jack Brooks Park (Hitchcock, TX), Resistol Arena (Mesquite, TX), Will Rogers Memorial Center (Fort Worth, TX), and Perth Ag Indoor Arena (Crockett, TX) to name a few.

Several notable changes within Soul Circuit/Subterranean Circuit rodeos, in the new millennium, have recently been identified vis-á-vis some of the research findings by the late C. Allen Haney and I in the 1990s. For example, computer technology is currently employed in many of the rodeos to market and promote upcoming shows (e.g., Facebook); register cowboys' entry fees; document scores; and play music throughout the competition. Some of the more established contemporary rodeo organizations like U2 Rodeo Promotions have even set up PayPal and Ticketron accounts, whereby spectators can purchase tickets online and select seats without standing in box office lines. Another unique aspect of the contemporary Soul Circuit/Subterranean Circuit rodeo is their affiliation with various sanctioning organizations to validate, corroborate, and maintain the respective guidelines of the sport. The most prominent sanctioning organization for Soul Circuit/

Subterranean Circuit rodeos has been the Anahuac Salt Grass Cowboys Association; however, rodeo legend Myrtis Dightman recently partnered with the Cowboys Professional Rodeo Association (CPRA) for his annual Hall of Fame Rodeo in Crockett, TX, which has been held for more than 30 years.

MARKETING MIX IMPLEMENTATION

The complexion as well as the mission of the Soul Circuit/Subterranean Circuit rodeos have changed somewhat over time. No longer are they primarily marketed to black cowboys trying to pick up pocket change over the weekend and their devotees. As Cleo Hearn, U2 Rodeo Productions founder and promoter, noted with regard to the Cowboys of Color Rodeo series: "We have a sellable commodity. We have marketable and quality cowboys competing—people of all colors" (personal interview, May 20, 2019). This family-owned and operated sport enterprise run by Hearn, his wife, and four sons, each having attended college on a rodeo scholarship, is the gold standard among minority-promoted rodeos in Texas. The Hearn family is involved in all aspects of the rodeo production including contract negotiation, marketing, event, and facility management. Cleo Hearn contends that the "black rodeos" or "All Colored" rodeos of the past are more integrated in the new millennium and thus requires a marketing strategy which encompasses a wider demographic. Therefore, U2 Rodeo Productions has placed considerable emphasis on what market researchers like McCarthy (1960) and Stier (2014) have referred to as the "4Ps," "4Ps Plus," or "Five Ps" (i.e., product, promotion, public, place, and price), the basic elements within marketing and their interrelatedness to quality event management. For example, the product (rodeo) is determined to a great extent by a number of factors related to the rodeo's structure. As a result, considerable time and effort are devoted to such things as the type of rodeo, athlete solicitation, registration process, rough stock caliber, venue selection, sponsorship, event entertainment, and vendor/concession placement. The invitational aspect of the Cowboys of Color rodeos also suggests a more upscale level of competition because contestants are individually solicited to compete. As would be expected, in invitational sport competitions, athletic prowess and past performance are major factors when invitations are extended. Yet, other variables like potential, demeanor, and notoriety are weighed as well. The Cowboys of Color Invitational Rodeo series culminates the season with its National Finals Rodeo held annually at the Resistol Arena in Mesquite, TX. Known for hosting major events in the Dallas Metroplex, the Resistol Arena is a PRCA-sanctioned venue where the Mesquite Championship Rodeo is annually held and televised.

The diversity and inclusion philosophy of U2 Rodeo Productions is primarily the rationale for the rodeo series being called *Cowboys of Color*. Hearn, who may be considered bi-racial due to his African American and Seminole Indian ancestry, contends that cowboys from diverse racial/ethnic backgrounds can feel welcomed in this more inclusive environment which is reflected in some of the scheduled activities at the rodeos. This more diverse and inclusive rodeo environment also has implications with respect to marketing, promotions, and sponsorships—all necessary aspects for mass appeal and corporate support. For the Cowboys of Color Invitational Rodeo series financial support and in-kind contributions have been garnered from conglomerates like Ford Motor Company, Air Products & Chemical, Inc., American Airlines, and Bank of America, as well as small local businesses in the Dallas metroplex. U2 Rodeo production is of the opinion that anyone in business who sells a product is a potential sponsor. The marketing pitch has taken the form of paid radio and television commercials, billboard and newspaper advertisements, website announcements and computer e-blasts, along with promotional calendars, and traditional hand bills. A form of market segmentation has been employed whereby commercial airtime has been purchased from selected Hispanic and Native American radios stations to promote Cowboys of Color Invitational rodeos within these specific communities. These contemporary marketing strategies have enabled U2 Rodeo Productions to lease the more upscale air-conditioned indoor rodeo arenas and attract some of the top local and national entertainers for pre- and post-rodeo entertainment. Even though ticket prices, depending upon seating preference, may be a bit higher than other minority rodeos, the quality of vendors and other amenities are perceived by spectators as adding value to the ticket purchase and the perception that it is a bargain; particularly at rodeos where a portion of the proceeds benefit nonprofit entities.

SOCIOCULTURAL CONSCIOUSNESS AND EDUCATION VIA RODEO

A more socially conscious and community-oriented image appears to be reflected in several of the contemporary Soul Circuit/Subterranean Circuit rodeos as demonstrated in their structured social programs and coordinated youth engagement activities with various educational, civic, and philanthropic organizations. For example, over the years U2 Rodeo Productions has been the quintessential leader in championing social and community engagement activities through rodeo. Promoted as the "largest multicultural rodeo tour in the country" (Cowboys of Color, 2008, p. 9) with the tag line pitch "Let us entertain you while we educate you" is not merely a marketing ploy. A glimpse at the information filled programs distributed at Cowboys of Color Invitational Rodeos corroborates their tag line pitch regarding education and entertainment which are intimately intertwined. Although rarely discussed in conventional American history textbooks, the legacies and contributions of ethnic minority stakeholders who traversed western plains are conveyed through various media. Contained in each year's colorful souvenir program is historical information highlighting the contributions of ethnic minorities in the expansion of the western frontier. Biographies of legendary figures and historical events enable individuals to reconnect with the past. Also included are descriptions of the various rodeo events and scoring procedures for spectators with limited rodeo exposure. Charro (Spanish cowboy) and Escaramuza (Spanish female-mounted drill team) exhibitions, Native American ceremonial dancers, and Buffalo Soldier encampments and reenactments in full regalia, help acquaint rodeo spectators with the legacy of these frequently marginalized western frontier inhabitants. At the culminating Cowboys of Color National Finals Rodeo a petting zoo, pony rides, and cultural entertainers are all part of the educational component within the admission fee.

Education and training of minority cowboys/girls have been major components of Soul Circuit/Subterranean Circuit rodeos over the years. Akin to "farm systems" in various sport forms (e.g., Major League Baseball) or a training ground for novice rodeo cowboys/girls to hone their respective rodeo skills for PRCA competition, the Soul Circuit/Subterranean Circuit offers much more. Various skills that may be overlooked in some of the more conventional training programs like interviewing skills, cowboy etiquette, personal development, and professional standards adherence are often addressed along with specific rodeo event technique clinics. Like their mainstream counterparts, the education, training, and development opportunities start early even though many minority rodeo cowboy "want to be"s rarely live in a rural or agrarian environment where livestock are readily accessible for practice. The mutton busting contest, as well as pee wee and junior barrel racing, breakaway, and tie-down roping events are scheduled to expose children to the sport of rodeo at an early age.

Soul Circuit/Subterranean Circuit rodeos have attempted to enhance cultural awareness and galvanize minority communities through educational opportunities, community engagement, and civic awareness activities. For example, the Harold Cash Living Legend Rodeos have not only provided scholarship support for "in need" college students but has honored and paid tribute to black cowboys past and present that contributed to the legacy of black rodeo. Myrtis Dightman's Hall of Fame Rodeos via CPRA sanctioning have attempted to prepare cowboys for mini-bull and bucking horse qualification for Las Vegas, while the U2 Rodeos have been involved in myriad community services and civic outreach programs. Along with its scholarship program, U2 Rodeo Productions has partnered with ICREA, Inc., a 501 (c) (3) educational nonprofit organization that provides teacher training in creative thinking and cultural history in North Texas public and private schools. They have also worked with community leaders in the Deputy Mayor's Teen Summit and law enforcement agencies through its rodeos to address some of the contemporary issues confronting minority youths: gang violence, teen pregnancy, juvenile delinquency, unemployment, health, nutrition, and professional attire tips. One of the recent Teen Summits included a multicultural film and music festival in addition to a Black History Rodeo with "Black Historical Moments" interjected during breaks in the rodeo. The sponsored activity, which was free to all teen participants, was heavily supported and promoted by Dallas area businesses. Similarly, in the Fall of 2009 two U2 Rodeo competitions were co-sponsored by D.A.R.E. (Drug Abuse Resistance Education) in an effort to highlight the dangers of drug use. These are but a few of the community-based activities and programs that demonstrate the rodeo organization's social consciousness and commitment to community involvement.

Arguably U2 Rodeo Productions' most enduring sociocultural contribution has been its museum support. On June 15, 2019, U2 Rodeo promoted the 31st Annual Texas Black Invitational Rodeo at the Fair Park Coliseum in Dallas, TX to support the African American Museum of Dallas. It also annually sponsors a Cowboys of Color Rodeo to benefit the National Multicultural Western Heritage Museum (formerly the National Cowboys of Color Museum and Hall of Fame) in Fort Worth, TX. In addition to the financial support, numerous artifacts and memorabilia have been donated to the museum collection by U2 Rodeo Productions' founder Cleo Hearn and other Cowboys of Color supporters. The NMWHMHF is the "brain-child" of Fort Worth, Texas, residents Jim and Gloria Austin. Established in 2001, the museum is a repository for the collection of historical artifacts and memorabilia. Throughout the year the NMWHMHF host oral presentations by guest historians, cultural heritage workshops, and Western History symposiums. Additionally, it annually inducts minority cowboys/girls and western frontier luminaries into the NMWHM Hall of Fame at its new facility in the Historic Fort Worth Stockyards and Exchange District.

THE NEW MILLENNIUM BLACK RODEO COWBOY

Black rodeo cowboys of the twenty-first century appear to be more resolute in their quest to be successful in the sport. Although they are products of a new and more inclusive society where fashion, technology, and economic resources facilitate greater access to notoriety, it is yet to be seen whether the "New Jack" black rodeo cowboy will make a mark at the highest level of rodeo competition. We do know that black rodeo cowboys currently riding the conventional Soul Circuit/Subterranean Circuit may have shunned the afro hairstyle for dreadlocks and "Jack Johnson" haircuts; mount their respective steeds with cellphone attached earbuds; and drive multiton trucks and horse trailers that have rarely been used for ranching and/or farming. Suffice to say, they have many of the things that their predecessors longed for but were not privy to in a less inclusive society.

However, as in the past, some of the same professional sport career inhibitors still restrict black rodeo cowboys today as noted by Babers (2014) and Pearson (2004): entry fees, quality horses, structured training opportunities, mentors, and sponsorship. As legendary roping champion Fred Whitfield stated in Wooden and Ehringer's *Wranglers, Roughstock, & Paydirt: Rodeo in America*, "There are a lot of black athletes with talent, but they're just not into rodeoing. There's a lot of good ropers around Houston. Most of them stay home because they lack confidence and finances to do this full time" (1996, p. 211). Such statements have been echoed for many years pertaining to solo entrepreneurial athletes who must often subsidize all aspects of their sport involvement. This is a sport deterrent, in general, and major obstacle in particular for black cowboys. Yet opportunities to hone skills for PRCA access through college rodeo scholarships are viable, as well as the efforts made by well-meaning veteran cowboys like Cleo Hearn, whose goal has been to create a rodeo series that will enable blacks, Native Americans, and Hispanics to hone their skills in preparation for PRCA level competition. "I want to graduate five or ten cowboys to the pro ranks every year" (Wooden & Ehringer, 1996 p. 211).

Hearn, once a celebrated calf roper influenced by the legendary cigar puffing Marvel Rodgers, and the collective NFR successes of Fred Whitfield, Corey Solomon, and Bud Ford in the event, anecdotally, may have contributed to what appears to be an upward trend in black rodeo cowboys' competition of choice. This assumption is due to the plethora of black calf ropers competing at Soul Circuit/Subterranean Circuit rodeos; so many that there are often slack competitions in the morning and after the evening rodeo has concluded. This appears to be a unique contemporary phenomenon in light of the increased expenses incurred traveling and feeding a horse, or possibly two, for competition, contrary to bull riders, saddle bronc, and bareback riders who have fewer overhead cost because they have no need to transport animals and/or lease them from other cowboys. They have more freedom and flexibility to travel because of the limited amount of equipment required to perform in their respective events. At several recent rodeos (e.g., Harold Cash's Living Legend Rodeo and Myrtis Dightman's Hall of Fame Rodeo), surprisingly, bull riding was not a scheduled event. This was most unusual since bull riding is traditionally the marquee event, which may be scheduled at the beginning and at the conclusion of the rodeo.

This phenomenon may be due, in part, to the career longevity factor. Quite possibly contemporary cowboys competing in the timed events such as tie-down and breakaway roping realize that they can stay in the sport much longer than those competing in the rough stock events where the body is subjected to considerable trauma. This career decision may suggest that timed event cowboys sacrifice the perceived "bravado," "machismo," and adulation often associated with rough stock event cowboys for longevity. The tradeoff is plausible even though the expenses incurred are greater. As one veteran cowboy mentioned, a breakaway roper can possibly compete into his 60s whereas rough stock cowboys are usually done by age 40.

The Soul Circuit/Subterranean Circuit rodeos are no longer the cultural galvanizer they once were in rural black communities and various Texas Gulf Coast metropolitan areas. Much like the Negro Leagues during segregated times, and prior to the passing of major civil rights legislation, Soul Circuit/Subterranean Circuit rodeos were an integral part of the black communal ecosystem. To some extent this is still the case in small rural agricultural hamlets in southeast Texas, but times have brought about change and the sociocultural significance once endemic in black communities fostered by Soul Circuit/Subterranean Circuit rodeos is a bygone phenomenon. Yet, vestiges of the past are maintained via various themed rodeos, trail rides, and campouts. A partial listing of annual Soul Circuit/Subterranean Circuit rodeos is listed in the Epilogue.

REFERENCES

Babers, M. C. (2014). *Black Cowboys and Black Masculinity: African American Ranchers, Rodeo Cowboys and Trailriders* (Master's thesis, Texas A&M University). Retrieved from https://oaktrust.library.tamu.edu/bitstream/handle/1969.1/154111/BABERS-THESIS-2014.pdf?sequence=1&isAllowed=y

Cowboys of Color (2008). *Cowboys of Color Invitational Rodeos: National Finals Rodeo* [Brochure]. Retrieved from www.cowboysofcolorrodeo.net

Mauch, R. (2017, July). No tying him down. *Mansfield Now Magazine.* Retrieved from https://nowmagazines.com/onlineeditions/editions/717mansfield.pdf

McCarthy, E. J. (1960). *Basic Marketing: A Managerial Approach.* Homewood, IL: Irwin.

Pearson, D. W. (2004). Shadow riders of the subterranean circuit: A descriptive account of Black rodeo in the Texas Gulf Coast region. *The Journal of American Culture, 27(2),* 190–198.

Professional Rodeo Cowboys Association. (2019). Biographies - Fred Whitfield. *PRCA.* Retrieved from http://www.prorodeo.com/prorodeo/cowboys/cowboy-biographies?id=1150

RODEOTAX.COM. The buck stops here – Corey Solomon. *PRCA*. Retrieved from https://www.prorodeo.com/prorodeo/cowboys/cowboy-biographies?id=1083

Russell, D. (2016). *Cowboys of Color*. Dallas, TX: Taylor Specialty.

Stier, W. E., Jr. (2014). *Sport Management: The Business of Sport* (3rd ed.). Boston, MA: American Press.

Wachter, P. (2016, October). Fred Whitfield and the black cowboys of rodeo. *The Undefeated*. Retrieved from https://theundefeated.com/features/fred-whitfield-and-the-black-cowboys-of-rodeo/

Whitfield, F., & Powers, T. (2014). *Gold Buckles Don't Lie: The Untold Tale of Fred Whitfield*. Columbia County, FL: Gold Buckle Productions.

Wooden, W. S., & Ehringer G. (1996). *Rodeo in America: Wranglers, Roughstock, & Paydirt*. Lawrence, KS: University Press of Kansas.

Woods, R. B. (2016). *Social Issues in Sport* (3rd ed.). Champaign, IL: Human Kinetics.

Chapter 9

Reliving the Past via Contemporary Trail Riding

Trail riding, as an ancillary component of rodeo, is a ritualistic contemporary reenactment of the mid-nineteenth-century trek across the western plains in pursuit of a viable homestead. This nostalgic cultural pastime engaged in by thousands of individuals throughout the year has gained considerable attention of late. However, the reenactment takes on a significant meaning in Texas at the annual Houston Livestock Show and Rodeo (HLSR) when cowboys/girls take to the highways and byways en route to Houston (TX) on horses, mules, and covered wagons. Since 1952, when the first trail ride was staged, Western culture enthusiasts and devotees have donned their cowboy/girl drag and prepared themselves for an often-arduous sojourn to downtown Houston. Those most familiar with ranching and livestock management will climb on their trusted steeds or into a vintage replica covered wagon destined for a number of predetermined campsite respites for the journey. The actual trail rides vary depending upon where the trail riding outfit is located. Some trail rides will last more than two weeks and cover over 350 miles, while averaging approximately 3 miles per hour on heavily traveled highways. For example, the Los Vaqueros Rio Grande Trail Riders start their sojourn at the border crossing from Reynosa, Mexico. According to the HLSR (Campbell, n.d.), more than 3,000 trail riders from eleven to thirteen associations annually participate in this signature rodeo event. However, major preparations must be made prior to getting on the road. Participation fees, which vary depending upon the organization, must be collected in advance to offset trail riding operating cost. Also, standard guidelines informing trail riders of basic attire, riding format and protocol, as well as personal behavior must be addressed. Logistically, transportation routes must be coordinated, highway permits obtained, police escorts arranged, scouts identified to monitor traffic patterns, overnight campsites established, and basic amenities determined and packed (e.g., food, water, tents, firewood, porta potties, etc.). Arrangements must also be made to care for the horses and mules. Therefore, up to date Coggins Papers are required to verify the health of the animals; a farrier required to trim hooves and replace horseshoes; and animal feed consisting of hay, grass, and various dietary concentrates must be packed for however long the trip will take.

The annual HLSR trail ride is a longstanding ritual, and has become so prominent that it has garnered national attention from such newspapers as the *New York Times*. Beat writer Ralph Blumenthal noted the avidity, passion, and deference toward this annual pilgrimage in an article titled "A Hummer Alongside a Horse? The Rodeo Must Be in Houston" (Blumenthal, 2004). It is standard procedure for Houstonians from diverse backgrounds and social strata to shed their conventional business attire for their Stetson hats, Lucchese boots, Roper shirts, Wrangler jeans, and Scully vests all in the name of "cowboying/cowgirling up" for Go Texan Day and the HLSR parade. Some even don replica sheriff and deputy badges. Annually over 34,000 individuals volunteer to work in various capacities during this 21-day event. Many have been known to request a temporary leave of absence or use vacation time to participate. Some school districts even refrain from punishing students for absences related to the trail ride and HLSR participation.

Currently, there are four organized and sanctioned African American trail riding organizations participating in the HLSR parade annually. They include the Prairie View Trailriders Association, Northeastern Trail Riders Association, Southwestern Trail Riders Association, and the Southwest Trail Riders Association. The Northeastern Trail Riders Association, initially part of the Prairie View Trailriders Association, was the second black trail riding association established. It was organized partly to represent black Creole cowboys from Louisiana. Other associated African American trail riding groups that make the trip to Houston but may not participate in the parade are the Sugar Shack Trailblazers and Black History Riders of America. Having been subjected to racial taunts, epithets, and discriminatory treatment over the years, African American trail riding organizations have endured and are now a fixture in the annual celebration. This coveted status is due mainly to the pioneering efforts of Prairie View Trailriders Association founders James Francies, Jr. and PRCA Hall of Fame bull rider Myrtis Dightman, Sr. Their organization, which was established in 1957 with the slogan "Ride with Pride," (Figure 9.1) is the oldest and largest African American trail riding association with anywhere between 270–525 riders (Campbell, n.d.; Mack, 2001). Prior to the 2017 HLSR trail ride, Prairie View Trailriders Association members were required to pay a $40.00 fee, provide insurance forms, and Coggins Papers before receiving their commemorative purple and yellow lettered badge, with the shining white diamond, which represented the association's 60-year anniversary. The ride to Houston, which averages 20 miles a day depending on traffic patterns, is usually a week long and covers approximately 107 miles.

Francies and Dightman, who are still actively involved in the association, can genuinely attest to the past discriminatory treatment and segregated campsite accommodations in route to Houston. During an evening respite at the Community Faith Church (Houston, TX) where the association was being recognized and honored with a filmed documentary (February 2, 2018), prior to their downtown campsite arrival, Francies spoke candidly about the discriminatory treatment. He mentioned how the Prairie View Trailriders were forced to camp in a remote region of Memorial Park (parade staging area), away from other trail riding groups and various park amenities. This discriminatory treatment, lamented Francies, limited communal fraternization, comingling, and the sharing of common Western cultural experiences.

In a casual conversation with James Francies, Jr. several years later, he recanted a trail riding experience en route to the HLSR in 1963. He stated during his tenure as trail boss guiding the group down the highway, unbeknownst to many, the media did not mention the phalanx of National Guard, Department of Public Safety, Houston Police Department, and Sheriff's Department officers dispatched to escort and protect the trail riders from possible civil unrest. This became necessary due to the mounting civil unrest over segregation and discriminatory practices nationally. Law enforcement

Figure 9.1 Prairie View Trailriders Association Logo. *Source:* Courtesy of Myrtis Dightman, Jr. and Sherrie Johnson, 2014.

Figure 9.2 Francies, Dightman, and Cash. James Francies, Jr. (l), Myrtis Dightman, Sr. (c), and Harold Cash (r) at Community Faith Church, February 2, 2018. *Source:* Courtesy of Demetrius Pearson.

actually set up camp in close proximity to the Prairie View Trailriders Association campsite throughout their stay. Fortunately, there were no incidents of violence. However, in spite of the dangers, past social indignities and complexities of coordinating the annual event, both founders Francies and Dightman, Sr. (Figure 9.2) have been committed over the years to participate in the annual Rodeo Houston's Go Texan Day and parade, as well as maintaining the legacy of the black western homesteader, ranch hand, and rodeo cowboy.

The Prairie View Trailriders Association has been lauded through the years for its community service contributions and philanthropic endeavors. As a designated 501(c)(3) nonprofit organization, they annually award scholarships to Texas residents and Prairie View A&M students. Their devotion to preserving Texas culture and Western heritage, as well as educating students, has garnered financial support from the HLSR, which has pledged over $500,000 toward the Prairie View Trailriders Association's scholarship program. Not surprising the HLSR recognized them in 1986 as the best trail ride for that year, the highest honor bestowed upon a participating trail riding organization

In light of the accepted hardships (i.e., inclement weather, traffic congestion, covered wagon repairs, and animal re-shoeing) during this self-imposed western sojourn, trail riders take pride in the nostalgic atmosphere of the nightly campfires, chuck wagon meals, and lively Texas tunes. Whether live or pre-recorded the sounds of Country, Country and Western, Rhythm and

Blues, Zydeco Hip Hop, Rap, and Folk music fill the air. Yet, one would be remiss if cowboy cuisine were not mentioned. Although beans, brisket, and ribs are traditional Texas fare staples, much like Tex-Mex dishes (e.g., chili, burritos, enchiladas, etc.), Cajun/Creole food including jambalaya, boudin/boudain, fried catfish, crawfish, and gumbo have become chuck wagon favorites on the African American trail rides. This is due in part to the early Creole settlers in Spanish Texas around 1803 and the large contingent of former enslaved blacks that relocated to southeast Texas from Louisiana after the Civil War, and during the "Great Migration" of the early twentieth century (Pruitt, 2005, 2013; Steptoe, 2015). Arguably the most notable and accomplished chuck wagon cook among black trail riders is Nathan Jean Whitaker Sanders, fondly known as "Mama Sugar." She readily admits that following behind the rear end of a horse or mule was not overly appealing but took to trail riding because of her six daughters' fascination with the experience. This was the impetus for Mama Sugar establishing the Sugar Shack Trailblazers in 1983 at her ranch in nearby Fresno, TX. Yet, it's Mama Sugar's cooking that keeps her on the chuck wagon. She is so revered and accomplished as a cook that she has her own unpublished recipe book (*Mama Sugar Recipes*) and has contributed to several national publications (e.g., *Gourmet, The Texas Cowboy Cookbook*, etc.) on Texas cuisine. It is not polite to share a woman's age; however, let's say Mama Sugar has logged many a mile on the trail satisfying the palates of hungry cowboys and cowgirls.

As mentioned previously, the trail ride to Houston for the HLSR's Go Texan Day and parade is a big deal. It is obviously more than grown-ups donning Western attire and romanticizing about the Old West. It actually represents a deeper passion, understanding, and cultural appreciation for the ranching pioneers who braved the elements to make southeast Texas a celebrated livestock producer. The trail riders' pilgrimage to the annual HLSR attests to their deference and devotion to westward expansion, livestock management, and the ranching spirit passed down through generations. It is literally a cultural experience that is serious business—culturally and financially.

REFERENCES

Blumenthal, R. (2004, March 1). A hummer alongside a horse? The rodeo must be in Houston. *New York Times*. Retrieved from https://www.nytimes.com/2004/03/01/us/a-hummer-alongside-a-horse-the-rodeo-must-be-in-houston.html

Campbell, D. (n.d.). Their happy trails blazed pathways of respect and historic achievements for African-Americans. *African American News & Issues*. Retrieved from http://www.aframnews.com/prairie-view-trail-riders-association/traditions in Southeast Texas. *Journal of Religion and Popular Culture 26*(1), 124-143.

Houston Livestock Show and Rodeo (n.d.). *The Spirit of the Volunteer*. Retrieved from http://volunteers.rodeohouston.com/

Mack, K. (2001, February 9). For 43 years, black cowpokes "ride with pride" to the rodeo. *The Houston Chronicle*. Retrieved from https://www.chron.com/news/article/For-43-years-black-cowpokes-ride-with-pride-to-2006745.php

Pruitt, B. (2005, Fall). In search of freedom: Black migration to Houston, 1914–1945. *The Houston Review of History and Culture, 3*(1), 45–57, 85–86.

Pruitt, B. (2013). *The Other Great Migration: The Movement of Rural African Americans to Houston, 1900-1941*. College Station, TX: Texas A&M Press.

Steptoe, T. (2015, December 15). When Louisiana Creoles arrived in Texas, were they black or white? *Zócalo*. Retrieved from http://www.zocalopublicsquare.org/2015/12/15/when-louisiana-creoles-arrived-in-texas-were-they-black-or-white/ideas/nexus/

Epilogue

This project is but one square in the legacy quilt of the black rodeo cowboy, whose experiences in mainstream rodeo and the Soul Circuit/Subterranean Circuit, in particular, have not been forgotten. Writing and discussing the many aspects pertaining to black cowboys in general, and black rodeo cowboys in the Texas Gulf Coast Region in particular, have been most interesting. Their collective stories and experiences are all a part of American history which has often been neglected and erased from our collective consciousness. This is partly due to what Wooden and Ehringer (1996) stated about the status of black rodeo cowboys. They maintain that for many years blacks were viewed as "outsiders" in rodeo (p. 209).

The contents of this book have been derived from 20 years of work and numerous hours in the field conducting research and learning about this unique cultural phenomenon called rodeo. The myriad activities included participant and nonparticipant observing; interviewing rodeo participants and spectators; examining sundry rodeo artifacts and memorabilia in select archives and personal collections; and an extensive literature review of most everything available regarding African American rodeo involvement in the Texas Gulf Coast Region. However, I would be naïve to think that this work is the panacea and epitome of the research on the topic. Suffice to say, this book represents a mere patch in the quilt of American rodeo history. As exhaustive, time consuming, and tedious as this project has been it pales in contrast to what the black cowboys I talked about endured over the years. I am honored to help bring their storied past to light.

Although researchers in the humanities and social sciences have begun to take more of an interest in this sociocultural phenomenon over the past 50 years, their writings have had but a modicum impact on the many faces of the American cowboy as well as those who compete in their prole sport of choice—rodeo. A concerted effort must be made to document the untold history of black livestock managers (i.e., ranch hands and herders) and rodeo cowboys who were often denied opportunities to compete and excel in the rodeo arena. Their involvement in various occupations on the American Western frontier was invaluable during its expansion, yet they are rarely depicted in books, films, paintings, prints, and photographs. As a result, black cowboys have become an invisible aspect of the American West and its most celebrated frontier—Texas. This perception has been inculcated into the American psyche so much so that today's black youth are not often aware of the existence and contributions of black cowboys to Western heritage, and even fewer actually understand what they meant to cowboying and livestock management. It was for good reason noted Harlem Renaissance poet Langston Hughes urged historian William Katz not to leave out the black cowboy in his African American history text shortly before his death in 1967. Ironically, the frontier has been said to have helped shape American democracy, yet this perspective overlooked, marginalized, and completely ignored the meaningful contributions made by a segment of its stakeholders—African Americans. Unfortunately, we are resigned to live with the words of Weston (1985): "Our Western myth began to form early on the very frontier it presented and shaped—and from the beginning excluded blacks" (p. 153).

REFERENCES

Weston, J. (1985). *The Real American Cowboy.* New York, NY: Schocken Books.
Wooden, W. S., & Ehringer G. (1996). *Rodeo in America: Wranglers, Roughstock, & Paydirt.* Lawrence, KS: University Press of Kansas.

Appendix

SELECT BLACK RODEO RESOURCE SITES AND REPOSITORIES

The Black Cowboy Museum
1104 3rd Street
Rosenberg, Texas 77471
(281) 787- 3308
www.TheBlackCowboyMuseum.otg

American Cowboy Museum
Taylor-Stevenson Ranch
11822 Almeda Road
Houston, TX 77045
(713) 478-9677
www.americancowboymuseum.org

National Multicultural Western Heritage Museum
2029 North Main Street
Fort Worth, TX 76164
(817) 534-8801
www.cowboysofcolor.org

Cowtown Coliseum
(Texas Rodeo Cowboy Hall of Fame)
121 E. Exchange Avenue
Fort Worth, TX 76164
1-(800) Cowtown
www.cowtowncoliseum.org

Texas Cowboy Hall of Fame
128 E. Exchange Avenue
Fort Worth, TX 76164
(817) 626-7131
info@texascowboyhalloffame.org

Amon Carter Museum of American Art
3501 Camp Bowie Blvd.
Fort Worth, TX 76107
(817) 738-1933
https://www.cartermuseum.org/

George Ranch Historical Park
10215 FM762 Rd.
Richmond, TX 77469
(281) 343-0218
info@georgeranch.org

Texas City Museum
1867 Settlement Historic District
117 S. Bell Drive
Texas City, TX 77591
https://texastimetravel.oncell.com/en/texas-city-1867-settlement-historic
 -district-134315.html

South Central Texas Rodeo Connection
SC TX Ring of Honor
Dripping Springs Ranch Park
1042 Event Center Drive
Dripping Springs, TX 7860
(512) 858-4725
http://www.sctxrodeo.com/index.html

UTSA Institute of Texan Cultures
801 E. Cesar Chavez Blvd.
San Antonio, TX 78205-3296
(210) 458-2300
https://texancultures.utsa.edu/?q=rdr

Prairie View A&M University
Special Collections
John B. Coleman Library
P.O. Box 519, MS 1040

Prairie View, TX 77446
(936) 261-1500
http://www.pvamu.edu/

PARTIAL LISTING OF NOTABLE BLACK RODEOS

1st Annual George Ranch Rodeo to Honor Fort Bend County's Black Cowboy Legacy
George Ranch Historical Park
Richmond, TX 77469
February 16, 2019

14th Annual SE Henderson Memorial Rodeo
Henderson Arena
Egypt, TX 77434
April 14, 2019

31st Texas Black Invitational Rodeo
State Fair Coliseum
Fair Park, TX 75210
June 15, 2019

Juneteenth & Father's Day Rodeo
Circle M Arena
Fresno, TX 77545
June 20, 2019

Independence Day Celebration Rodeo
Circle M Arena
Fresno, TX 77545
July 6, 2019

R.V. Ranch Rodeo
R. V. Ranch
McBeth, Texas 77515
July 27, 2019

Liz Cook Riding Club 25th Annual Campout, Trailride, and Rodeo
Colorado County Fairground
Columbus, TX 78934
August 2, 2019

1st Prickly Pear Rodeo
Fort Bend County Fairgrounds
Rosenberg, TX 77471
August 17, 2019

Harold Cash Living Legend Rodeo
Jack Brooks Park Rodeo Arena
Hitchcock, TX 77563
August 24, 2019

Myrtis Dightman Hall of Fame Rodeo
Porth Ag Indoor Arena
Crockett, TX 75835
August 31, 2019

29th Annual Labor Day Rodeo & Trailride
Circle M Arena
Fresno, TX 77545
September 1, 2019

Solomon & Family Rodeo
28th Annual Open Timed Event Rodeo
Williams Ranch
Hempsted (Monaville), TX
September 14, 2019

38th Annual Glover's Rodeo, Campout & Trail Ride
Robertson County Fairgrounds
Hearn, TX 77859
September 21, 2019
R.V. Ranch Rodeo
Ranch Rodeo
McBeth, TX 77515
September 28, 2019

Cowboys of Color Invitational Rodeo
Mesquite Arena
Mesquite, TX 75149
November 2, 2919

Index

Note: Page numbers in italic denotes figure.

1st Annual George Ranch Rodeo to Honor Fort Bend County's Black Cowboy Legacy, 115
1st Prickly Pear Rodeo, 116
14th Annual SE Henderson Memorial Rodeo, 115
29th Annual Labor Day Rodeo & Trailride, 116
31st Texas Black Invitational Rodeo, 101, 115
38th Annual Glover's Rodeo, Campout & Trail Ride, 116

African American ancestral involvement, 17–22; livestock management, 17–22. *See also* cattle herding
African American Cowboy – The Forgotten Man of the West documentary, 38
The Age of Exploration, 2, 75
Ali, Muhammad, 50
All-American Rodeo Association, Anahuac Southwestern National Cowboy Association (SWNCA), 38
All-American Rodeo Association Bare Back, 51

All-Around Championship, 52
All-Around Cowboy, 52
Allen, M., 7, 44
American Black Cowboy Association, 50
American Cowboy Museum, xi, 113
The American West: Interactions, Intersections, and Injunctions (Bakken and Farrington), 25
Anahuac Saltgrass Cowboy's Association (ASGCA), 38, 56
Angelle, Denny, 41
Antonio, San, xiii
archival research, x
Arena, Resistol, 97
Arena Legacy (Rattenbury), 8
ASGCA. *See* Anahuac Saltgrass Cowboy's Association (ASGCA)
Athearn, R. G., 24
Austin, Moses, 11–15
Austin, Stephen F., 11–12, 15
Austin's colony during reconstruction, 20–22
Autry, Gene, 80

Babers, M. C., 102
Bad Ones, 51

Barr, Alwyn, 13, 17, 26
Barrett, Hadley, 57
Battle of San Jacinto, 14
Beaver, Joe, 44, 94
Becher, M., 25
Beckwourth, James, 76
Before Emancipation: Black Cowboys and the Livestock Industry (Liles), 17
Believe in Tomorrow Children's Foundation, 93
Bell, Alexander Graham, 29
Best Judged Roping Horse, 51
Bill, Buffalo, 7
Bill, Cherokee, xiii
Black, Red and Deadly: Black and Indian Gunfighters of the Indian Territories, 1870–1907 (Burton), xiii
The Black Cowboy Museum, 45, 59, 113
black cowboys and western frontier, 27–28
Black Cowboys In The American West: On the Range, On the Stage, Behind the Badge (Glasrud and Searles), 23, 25, 28
Black Cowboys of Texas (Massey), 11
Black Gun, Silver Star: The Life and Legend of Frontier Marshal Bass Reeves (Burton), xiii
Black Heritage Night, 57
Black History Riders of America, 106
Black History Rodeo, 101
black in the saddle, 75–89; competition, 83–85; down the rodeo trail, 81–82; institutionalized marginalization, 76–78; rodeo venues and arbitrary gatekeepers, 82–83; shadow riders, 76–78
black rodeo and New Jack cowboys, 91–103; education via rodeo, 99–101; flag bearers, 92–97; marketing mix implementation, 98–99; new millennium black rodeo cowboy, 101–3; new normal, 97–98; sociocultural consciousness, 99–101

black rodeo cowboy, 33–59; ancillary components, 54–59; emergence, 33–59; parallel paths, cultural context of, 39–40; soul circuit legacy, 40–48; in Texas Gulf Coast, early years, 37–39
Black Rodeo documentary, 50
Black Rodeo in the Texas Gulf Coast Region: Charcoal in the Ashes (Pearson), xiv
Black Texas: A History of African Americans in Texas (Barr), *1528–1995*, 13
Black West (Katz), 13, 25
Blumenthal, Ralph, 106
Blumer, Herbert, x
Boston Red Sox, 80
Bronco Band, 58
Broussard, Albert, 25
Brown, Freckles, 46, 87
Buck, Rufus, xiii
The Bull Dogger, 33, *34*
bulldogging (steer wrestling), 8, 63
bullfighting, 2
bull riding guru, 41
Burton, Art, xiii
Butler, George Washington, 26

cala de caballo (horse reining), 6
Calf Roping With Rufus Green: Fact or Fiction (Lawson), *43*
Callies, Larry, 58
Carlson, Paul, 3–4
Carrizales, Omar, 43
Cash, Harold, 48, 51–52
cattle herding, 17–22; George Ranch, 20–22; in Northern Africa, 18; in sub-Saharan areas of Africa, 17
cattle ranching and, 11–15
chaparreras (chaps), 5
churros, 7
Civil Rights Act of 1964, 39, 41, 45
Civil Rights Act of 1968, 39
Cleveland, Paul, 48, 51
Coakley, J. J., 33, 62
coleadero (tailing the bull), 5, 7

The Colonizer (Tracy and Havelock-Bailie), 11
Color Invitational Rodeo cowboy, 100
Color Rodeo, 50
contemporary trail riding, 105–9; reliving the past via, 105–9
Corey Solomon, 102
Course Landaise, 2
Cowboys of Color Invitational Rodeo, 40, 50, 67, 95, 98, 116
Cowboys of Color National Finals Rodeo, 100
Cowboys of Color pictorial, 91
Cowboys of Color Rodeo, 40, 50, 67, 95, 98–101
Cowboys Professional Rodeo Association (CPRA), 98
The Cowboy Way: An Exploration of History and Culture, 3
Cowtown Coliseum, 35, 50, 113
The Crimson Skull, 33
criollo (Spaniards born in North America), 5
Crow, Jim, 45, 55, 64–65, 92
Cy Young Award, 85

D.A.R.E. (Drug Abuse Resistance Education), 101
Deeringer, Martha, 29
DeLeon, Arnoldo, 7
de Narváez, Pánfilo, xiii
Denver National Western Stock Show, 50
Dightman, Myrtis, 38, 45–48, *48*, 53, 55, 77, 85, 88, 94, 98, 100
Dightman, Myrtis, Sr., 106, *108*
Dorantes, Andres, xiii
Downs, Manor, 43
Durham, P., 27

education via rodeo, 99–101
Ehringer, Gavin, 44, 111
Elizabethan Era, 75
Elliot, Dustin, 93
Emancipation Proclamation, 20, 78

Emmons, Johnny, 95
Escaramuza (Spanish female-mounted drill team), 100
ethnographic research, x
etiological aspects, rodeo roots and, 1–9; Bronze Age (3000–1100 B.C.), 1; evolution, 1–3; Mexican origins, 3–4; work-related pastime, 4–9

Fishwick, M. W., 24
floreo de reata (making flowers of rope), 7
Floyd Frank Rodeo Arena, 38
Ford, Bud, 92, 94, 102
Fort Bend County, 78
Fort Worth Fat Stock Show and Rodeo, 78
Fort Worth Stock Show, 52, 94
Francies, James, Jr., 106, 107, *108*
Francis, James, 46
Frank, Floyd, 38
Fredriksson, K., 8
Fred Whitfield, 102

Garrison, Zina, 91
Geo, x
George Ranch Historical Park, xi, 75, 114
Gilbert, Mary, 33
Glasrud, B. A., 23, 28
Glass, Dick, xiii
Glover, Melvin, 56
Glover Legacy Rodeos, 56
Gold Buckles Don't Lie: The Untold Tale of Fred Whitfield (Whitfield), 95
Gonzalez, Clarence, 42–43
Gordon, Freddie Skeet, 49
Greely, Calvin, Jr., 44
Green, Rufus, Sr., 38, 43–44
Guerrero, Vincente, 13–14
Guice, John D. W., 17–18

Hall, Taylor, Jr., 48–49
Hamilton, Kenneth Marvin, 26

Handbook of Texas Online (Carrizales), 43
Haney, C. Allen, 97
Harold Cash Living Legend Rodeo, 51, 100, 116
Harrison, N. K., 24
Hatfield, Mark, 55
Hearn, Cleo, 48, 50, 95, 98, 102
herraderos (branding), 5
The Hispanic Influence on the History of Rodeo (LeCompte), 7
HLSR. *See* Houston Livestock Show & Rodeo (HLS&R)
Hofmann, R. J., 8
Holmes, Neil, 93, 94
Holt, Susan Avera, 49
hoolihanding, 36
Houston Fat Stock Show, 43
Houston Hobby Center, 51
Houston Livestock Show & Rodeo (HLS&R), 51, 55, 57, 78, 94, 95, 105
Hughes, Langston, 112

Iber, Jorge, 3
Independence Day Celebration Rodeo, 115
In Search of the Racial Frontier: African Americans in the American West 1528–1990 (Taylor), 26

Jackson, A., 19
Jackson, E., Jr., 63, 77
Jackson, Robert, 56
James, Will, 24
Jefferson, Thomas, 15
jineteos de toros (bull riding), 6
Johnson, Grant, xiii
Johnson, Smitty, 57
Jones, Bob, 21
Jones, E. L., 27
Jones, Henry, 12, 14, 19–20
Jones, Kathryn, 50
Jones-Ryon plantation (ranch), 20
Jr. Roping, 71
Juneteenth & Father's Day Rodeo, 115

Junior Roping (18 and under), 71

Kanew, Jeff, 49–50
Katz, W. L., 13, 27, 112
Kuyendall, Joseph, 19

land acquisition in Austin's colony, 11–15; cattle ranching and, 11–15; slave labor and Mexican government, 13–15
Lawrence, E. A., 63
Lawson, Monroe W., 43
lazo (lasso), 5
LeCompte, Mary Lou, 7
Let's Go, Let's Show, Let's Rodeo: African Americans And The History Of Rodeo essay (Patton and Schedlock), 24
Liles, Deborah M., 17
livestock management, 17–22. *See also* cattle herding
The Living Legend Hall of Fame, 52
Liz Cook Riding Club 25th Annual Campout, Trailride, and Rodeo, 115

Madison County Fairgrounds Arena, 56
Madison Square Garden, 85
Manley, Effa, 39
Mansfield Now Magazine (Ford), 94
marketing mix implementation, 98–99
Martin, George, 20
Martin, Peter, 14, 19, 21
Martin, Wily, 12–14, 19
Martinez, Antonio, 11
Massey, Sara, 11
Mayfield, Sylvester, 52
McCarthy, E. J., 98
McQueen, Steve, 48
Mead, George Herbert, x
Mesquite Championship Rodeo, 98
mestizo, 5
Mexican government, slave labor and, 13–15
Mexican origins, 3–4
Miller, Zeke, xiii

Miller Brothers' 101 Ranch Real Wild West Show, 8, 33–34
Mitchell, Blue, 94
Mitchell, Ezekiel, 92, 93
Mix, Tom, 34
The Modern Black Cowboy (Morris), 91
Moffitt, Don, 95
Moffitt, Roy, 95
Moore, M. R., 11–12, 17, 21, 75
Morse, Samuel, 29
Mutton Busting (5 and 6), 71
Myrtis Dightman Hall of Fame Rodeo, 116
mythical west, 23–30; black cowboys and western frontier, 27–28; cattle drives, 23–30; cowboys, 23–30; invisible cowboys in a fading industry, 29–30
The Mythic West in the Twentieth-Century America (Athearn), 23

National Cowboy Hall of Fame, 85
National Cowboys Rodeo Association (NCRA), 38
National Finals Rodeo (NFR), 52–53, 57, 85, 94, 96, 98, 102
National High School Rodeo finals, 52, 57
National Intercollegiate Rodeo Association (NIRA), 52
National Multicultural Western Heritage Museum, xi, 39, 97, 101, 113
National Multicultural Western Heritage Museum and Hall of Fame (NMWHMHF), 41, 43–44, 49, 52, 54, 57, 101
Navaira, Emilio, 58
NCRA. *See* National Cowboys Rodeo Association (NCRA)
Negro League Baseball, 39–40, 42, 55
Negro Leagues, x, 71–72, 77–78, 103
The Negro Motorist Green Book, 54
Nelson, Steve, 20
new millennium black rodeo cowboy, 101–3

Newark Eagles, 39
Newman, A., 25
NIRA. *See* National Intercollegiate Rodeo Association (NIRA)
Northeastern Trail Riders Association, 106

Ohl, Cody, 94, 97
Old Glory Blow Out, 7
Old Time Rodeo Association, 51–52
Old Timers Roping (40 and over), 71
Open (Elite competition), 71
Open Break-Away event, 71
Oropeza, Vincente, 7

Paige, Satchel, 85
Park, Jack Brooks, 97
Patton, T. O., 24
Paul, George, 87
Pawnee Bill's Historic Wild West, Colonel Tim McCoy's Real Wild West, 8
Pearson, D. W., 102
Pee Wee (13 and under), 71
Perry, Jim, 27
Pickett, Bill, 33, 63, 76, 77, 95
Pickett, Thomas Jefferson, 33, *35*
Pickett Brothers Bronco Busters, 30, 33
Platt, North, 7
Poindexter, Alfred, 55
Pollard, Fritz, 80
Porter, K. W., 2
Prairie View, TX 77446, 55, 92, 94, 115
Prairie View A&M University, 55, 64, 92, 94, 108, 114
Prairie View Trail Riders Association, 47, 55, 106–8
PRCA. *See* Professional Rodeo Cowboys Association (PRCA)
PRCA Bull Riding World Championship, 47
Professional Bull Riders (PBR), 62, 92–94

Professional Rodeo Cowboys
  Association (PRCA), 37, 62–65, 69–
  72, 77, 80–82, 87, 92, 94–102, 106
ProRodeo Hall of Fame, 34, 44, 57, 76,
  97
pun'kin rollers, 38
Ranch, George, 20–22, 40, 59, 78, 80,
  97
Ranch, McFaddin, 38
rancho (farm), 5
Ratjen, Jack, 95
Rattenbury, R. C., 8
Raye, Collin, 58
RCA. *See* Rodeo Cowboys Association
  (RCA)
The Real American Cowboy (Weston),
  xi
Reeves, Bass, xiii
Richard, Jim, Jr., 57
Richardson, Freddie, 42
Richardson, Sherman, 42
Rider, Bull, 88
Robbins, A., 25
Robertson, Cliff, 48
Robinson, Jackie, 83
Rodeo Cowboy Hall of Fame, 57
Rodeo Cowboys Association (RCA), 37,
  40–41, 43, 45–46, 49, 51
*Rodeo Cowboys in the North American
  Imagination* (Allen), 7
Rodeo Handbill, 68
Rodeo in America (Wooden and
  Ehringer), 44, 102
Rogers, Marvel, 44, 50, 102
Rogers, Will, 34
Rough Riders, 30
Rough Riders Association, 33
Russell, Charles, 24
Russell, Don, 91
R.V. Ranch Rodeo, 56, 115
Ryon, Polly, 21
Ryon, William, 20

Sampson, Charles "Charlie," 47, 53–54,
  77, 94, 96

San Fermin fiesta, 2
Schedlock, S. M., 24
Searles, M. N., 23, 28
shadow riders of subterranean circuit,
  61–72, 76–78; financial constraints,
  70; historical review, 62–63;
  institutionalized marginalization,
  76–78; job stability concerns,
  70; marketing and promotional
  strategies, 67–69; meticulous record
  keeping, 70; rodeo and Americana,
  62–63; rodeo competitions, 69–70;
  rodeo venues, 66–67; soul circuit
  setting, 64; Soul Circuit/Subterranean
  Circuit, 61, 62, 64, 67, 70–72;
  sponsorship, 70; vendor fees, 70
Shoulders, Jim, 87
Silver Spurs Rodeo, 94
slave labor and Mexican government,
  13–15
Smith, Jim, 57
SNCA. *See* Southwestern National
  Cowboys Association (SNCA)
Social Issues in Sport (Woods), 91
sociocultural consciousness, 99–101
Solomon, Corey, 92, 94
Solomon, Larry, Sr., 94
Solomon & Family Rodeo, 116
Soul Circuit competition, x, 38, 61,
  64–69, 71, 81
soul circuit legacy, 40–48
soul circuit setting, 64
Soul Circuit/Subterranean Circuit, xiii,
  xiv, 12, 38, 43–45, 49, 51–58, 67–68,
  70–72, 93–95, 97–103
South Central Texas Rodeo Connection,
  114
South Central Texas (SC TX) Rodeo
  Ring, 41, 45, 49–50
Southwest Colored Cowboys
  Association, 50
Southwestern Colored Cowboys
  Association (SCCA), 37, 63, 77
Southwestern National Cowboys
  Association (SNCA), 37–38, 56

Southwestern Trail Riders Association, 106
Southwest Trail Riders Association, 106
Sports in Society: Issues and Controversies (Coakley), 33
Stahl, Jesse, 33, 35–36, *36*, 77
Stampede, Calgary, 52
The Stampede by Lightning or *The Stampede* (Remington), 23
steer wrestling, 2, 5, 8, 30, 34, 49, 56, 63
Stier, W. E., Jr., 98
Strode, Woody, 50
Subterranean Circuit, x, 38, 52, 61, 63. *See also* shadow riders of subterranean circuit
Sugar Shack Trailblazers, 106, 109
symbolic interactionism, x

Tallman, Bob, 57
Taureador Fresco, 1–2
Taylor, Quintard, 26
Tejas, 14
Texas Bull Riding Hall of Fame, 57
Texas City Museum, 114
Texas Cowboy Hall of Fame, 30, 97, 114
Texas Gulf Coast, early years, 37–39
Texas High School Rodeo Championship, 52
Texas Revolution, 12–14
Texas Rodeo Cowboy Hall of Fame, 40, 44, 49, 57, 80, 83, 87, 113
They Called Them Greasers (DeLeon), 7
Thomas, Willie, 38, 40–42, *42*, 46, 49, 51, 78–87, *79*, *88*; pioneer of sorts, 78–81; unheralded celebrity, 78–81

Thompkins, Harry, 44, 86–87
Treaties of Velasco, 14
Tritt, Travis, 58

U2 Rodeo Productions, 50, 97, 99, 101
The Undefeated, 96
UTSA Institute of Texan Cultures, 114

vaca (cow), 5–6
vaquero (cowboy), 5–7
venues, rodeo, 66–67; concession stands, 66; Soul Circuit rodeo venues, 66; Spartan, 66; spectator amenities, 66

Wainwright (Alberta) Stampede, 94
Walker, A. J., 56
Wallace, Christian, 45
Warren, Jonah, 57
Watkins, Thayer, 3
Watriss, Wendy, x
western colorphobia, 27–28
Weston, J., xi, 18, 23, 25, 27
Whitfield, Fred, 44, 77, 92, 94–96, 102
Wild Horse Race Championship, 42, 49
Wild West Show, 7, 76
Willeby, Krystal, 41
Williams, Preacher, 57
Williams, Sloan, 58
Williams, Tex, 48, 52, 58
Wood, P. H., 18
Wooden, W. S., 44, 111
Woods, Robert, 91
work-related pastime, rodeo as, 4–9
Wranglers Roughstock, & Paydirt: Rodeo in America (Wooden and Ehringer), 102
Wyche, Clinton, 45

About the Author

Demetrius W. Pearson, EdD, is a tenured associate professor in the Sport and Fitness Administration Program, and formerly associate chair, in the Department of Health and Human Performance at the University of Houston. His research areas have focused on the sociocultural and historical aspects of sport. For the past 20 years, he has conducted research and written about African American involvement in various sport forms, particularly North American rodeo, as well as their depiction in sport films. He currently maintains a repository listing of American sport films from 1930 to the present. Demetrius Pearson has published over sixty peer-reviewed research articles, book chapters, and conference abstracts. He was also one of the chapter contributors to Glasrud and Searles' award-winning book *Black Cowboys in the American West*, which won the Ray and Pat Browne Award for the Best Edited Collection in Popular Culture and American Culture in 2017. Demetrius Pearson holds professional memberships in the following organizations: North American Society for the Sociology of Sport (NASSS), North American Society for Sport Management (NASSM), Society of Health and Physical Educators (SHAPE America), and Texas Association for Health, Physical Education, Recreation and Dance (TAHPERD).

www.ingramcontent.com/pod-product-compliance
Lightning Source LLC
Chambersburg PA
CBHW020127010526
44115CB00008B/1007